Recipes For Relaxed Italian Eating

Recipes For Relaxed Italian Eating

Valentina Harris

photography by Francesca Yorke

CASSELL ILLUSTRATED

For Italian food devotees everywhere

I want to thank Robin and Anna for working with me through this book with such conviction and a sense of fun, and also Sasha for working so hard with me on preparing the recipes for photography.

First published in Great Britain in 2006 by Cassell Illustrated,
a division of Octopus Publishing Group Limited
2-4 Heron Quays, London E14 4JP

Distributed in the United States of America by
Sterling Publishing Co., Inc.,
387 Park Avenue South, New York, NY 10016-8810

A CIP catalogue record for this book is available from the
British Library.

ISBN-13: 978-1-844035-47-2
ISBN-10: 1-844035-47-6

10 9 8 7 6 5 4 3 2 1

Editor: Robin Douglas-Withers
Managing Editor: Anna Cheifetz
Art Editor: Sarah Rock

Printed in China

contents

introduction

Sometimes it feels good not to rush through every second of our life as though we had an urgent appointment. While convenience food is exactly that—convenient—I truly believe it is still possible to indulge oneself in the immense pleasure of taking one's time over the loving preparation of a special meal, or even just one favorite dish. That is, after all, why the Slow Food movement was originally created—as the antithesis to Fast Food and to uphold all that is right and good about food that is produced or grown in a time honored, unhurried fashion, with care, and pride.

To that end, the most important ingredient contained in this particular book is time. Time to research the best ingredients, purchase them and prepare them at a slow pace, to be able to put a meal on the table in hours, not minutes, and relax and enjoy every mouthful. *Recipes for Relaxed Italian Eating* is my personal tribute to the Slow Food movement and everything that it stands for.

The recipes are a collection of old-fashioned favorites, new interpretations of old dishes, and completely new ideas. I hope that you will make the time to enjoy the luxury of cooking food with love and care, so that you can experience the feeling that makes me want to go on and on cooking—there is nothing I know of that is quite so immediately gratifying as placing food cooked in this way in front of those I care for, and watching them enjoy it.

The principles of Italian cooking are very simple: find the best ingredients you can, as locally as possible; make sure they are in season; then cook them with reverent simplicity. Unlike French cooking, Italian food is all about unashamed emotion and I have many Italian friends who are literally moved to tears by a perfectly prepared plate of something as simple as pasta with a tomato sauce. It is, of course, never my intention to make you weep, but I hope that this book will in some small way help to remind you that in Italy, which is where Slow Food began after all, many people still live to eat, and not the other way around.

1 late breakfasts and any time brunches

Breakfast, so they tell us, is the most important meal of the day. In this collection of breakfast recipes, there is something for everyone, whether your preference is for a savory treat such as sweet tomatoes on crusty toast, or for something sweet and satisfying, like a dense cup of luxurious hot chocolate into which one can dip some freshly baked, warm brioche. Of course, nowhere is it written that we must have breakfast in the early hours of the morning—it can be a delicious meal at any time of the day, or come to think of it, the night too! In Italy we call this *la prima colazione*, with lunch being *la colazione*—so literally translated, breakfast becomes simply a precursor to lunch. I love breakfast and always try not to miss it, and though I do appreciate that sometimes it is hard to find time to cook and enjoy it properly, there are also occasions when nothing else will do!

Frittelle con la Frutta Cotta

Pancakes with Poached Fruits

La frutta cotta is one of those dishes you are given to eat in Italy because of a belief in its ultimate health–giving properties. It is delicious, but has connotations of nursery food and infancy that many might find difficult. Personally, I think it is no more like nursery fare than the often very delicious fish pie, and I am surprised at the resistance this sometimes arouses! This is a lovely brunch dish of firm stewed apples, pears, and other fruits tucked inside a warm, sugary pancake.

Serves 4

For the pancakes:

⅞ cup (100g) all-purpose white flour

pinch of salt

1 egg

1¼ cups (300ml) milk

about 5 tsp vegetable or sunflower oil

granulated sugar for dusting

a little lemon juice

crème fraîche or plain yogurt to serve

For the fruit:

2 small russet apples, peeled and quartered

2 firm plums or greengages, pitted and halved

1 large firm peach or nectarine, pitted and quartered

1 large pear, peeled and quartered

1 handful of raisins or golden raisins, soaked in the juice of 1 orange

grated rind and juice of ½ lemon

grated rind and juice of ½ orange

4 tbsp granulated sugar

Begin by making the pancake batter. Sift the flour and salt into a bowl, then make a well in the center. Break the egg into the well and begin to beat the flour into the egg, gradually adding the milk until you have a smooth batter. Stir in one teaspoon of the vegetable or sunflower oil. Transfer to a pitcher for ease of pouring, then leave to stand until needed. If you are leaving the batter overnight, remember to cover and refrigerate.

Next, prepare the fruit. Place all fruit in a sauté pan and mix with your hands to evenly distribute. Pour over the juice and rind and add two tablespoons of the sugar. Cover the pan and simmer gently, shaking the pan occasionally, for 10–15 minutes, until the fruit is soft. Transfer the fruit to a bowl to cool.

While the fruit cools a little, make the pancakes. Heat a shallow skillet with one teaspoon of vegetable or sunflower oil, swirling the oil to coat the pan thoroughly. As soon as it is hot and the pan is properly coated with oil, pour in one-quarter of the batter, tipping the pan from side-to-side to make sure the batter spreads evenly. Allow the batter to set, which should take a minute or so. Use a metal spatula or round-bladed knife to loosen the edges, then flip the pancake over and cook for a further minute, shaking the pan to keep the pancake loose, until set. Tip the pancake out on to a plate and continue to make 4 more pancakes, adding extra oil to the pan as necessary. Put the pancakes in a low oven to keep them warm while you make the next batch, with a sheet of nonstick baking parchment between each pancake to prevent them sticking together.

To serve, spoon some fruit into the center of each pancake, fold over the pancake to loosely close, sprinkle with the remaining 2 tablespoons of sugar and a little lemon juice. Serve with a little crème fraîche, or possibly even plain yogurt, on the side.

Torta Francese di Cigliege

Clafouti with Cherries (or Peaches or Apricots)

I will never forget the first time my mother made this for us. She used very sour, dark cherries from Lazio, called *visciole* in local dialect. The combination of the eggy, sweet unctuous batter and the sharpness of the cherries seemed at the time like one of the most delicious creations ever to have come out of her kitchen. This recipe is unashamedly French, full of eggs and cream and butter, and utterly wonderful to serve warm as part of a brunch, or as a simple dessert.

Serves 8
1¼ cups (300ml) milk
1 vanilla bean, split
3½ cups (500g) all-purpose white flour
1¾ cups + 2 tbsp (400g) superfine sugar
8 whole eggs, beaten
8 egg yolks
2 sticks (250g) unsalted butter, softened, plus a little extra for greasing the dish
1¼ cups (300ml) heavy cream
3½ tbsp (50ml) dark rum
1 tsp orange flower water
pinch of salt
2¼lb (1.2kg) cherries, peaches or apricots (pitted)
1 cup (100g) slivered almonds
1 tbsp confectioners' sugar

Warm the milk until just below boiling point with the vanilla bean, then set aside to infuse and for the vanilla bean to soften. Grease a 9-in (23-cm) ceramic quiche dish very thoroughly; set aside.

When the vanilla bean is soft, remove it from the milk. Sift the flour into a mixing bowl. Stir in the sugar, then add the whole eggs, egg yolks, butter, and cream. Stir in the vanilla-flavored milk, then add the rum, orange flower water, and salt and mix together very thoroughly. Pour the batter into the prepared dish and arrange the fruit in a single layer, cut side down, in the batter.

Place in a preheated oven, 375°F, and bake for about 40 minutes, until golden and set. Remove the clafouti from the oven and sprinkle the top with the slivered almonds, then sift over the confectioners' sugar. Return it to the oven for about 8 minutes, until the almonds are toasted and the sugar melts, then remove from the oven and set aside to cool a little. I always think this is best served just warm.

Frullato

Fruit Smoothie

I can remember very clearly making this one summer morning at home in Rome, for breakfast before school. Our early version of a blender, which looked remarkably similar to the many retro versions currently on sale, had a central rubberized stopper in the lid. I filled the pitcher and replaced the lid, but not the stopper! It took a long time to remove my breakfast from the ceiling, and I went to school hungry. I have been very careful, ever since. You can, of course, vary the fruit as you wish, although the bananas do help give a thicker texture.

Serves 2

1¾ cups (400ml) ice-cold milk (skim or full fat, as you like)
2 bananas
1 handful of strawberries, hulled
freshly squeezed juice of 2 oranges
2 peaches, peeled and pitted

Put the milk into the blender. Add the bananas and whiz until smooth and thick. Add the strawberries and the orange juice, whiz again and then add the peaches. Whiz once more, then pour into tall glasses and serve.

Yoghurt con la Frutta, il Miele e le Noci

Yogurt with Fruit, Honey, and Nuts

This is the breakfast that my old friend Yatti and I would enjoy while idling on the harborfront in Pollonia, on the island of Milos, many years ago. There was something about the blueness of the sea and the silver tamarisk trees that made the combination of the clean-tasting yogurt, the richness of the honey, and the sharp sweetness of the fruit and nuts especially delicious. For me, this recipe, just like so many others, is intrinsically caught up in my whimsical web of memories. It is food that has the ability to transport me.

Serves 1 or 2

½ cup (100g) thick, creamy Greek-style yogurt
1 large tbsp clear honey, ideally Greek
1 large, juicy, fresh peach, peeled and sliced
5 or 6 fresh walnuts, cracked and shelled

Put the yogurt in a bowl or large, stemmed wine glass. Spoon over half the honey. Add the peach slices and walnuts, then drizzle the remaining honey over the whole thing and it's ready to eat.

Ricotta a mo'di Zuppa Inglese

Whipped Ricotta with Fresh Berries

This is the kind of cool, refreshing addition to a summer breakfast table that always reminds me of how wonderful ricotta can be. If possible, use really fresh ewe's milk ricotta, as it has more flavor. In Sicily the local shepherd would bring us his ricotta every morning at breakfast, steaming hot and stinking of sheep. You can now get very good organic ricotta in most supermarkets or good cheese shops.

Serves 4

1lb (500g) fresh ricotta
3 tbsp superfine or confectioners' sugar
2 cups (300g) fresh, ripe berries, hulled if necessary, and rinsed
biscotti or slices of panettone or pandoro to serve

Place the ricotta in a bowl and use a balloon whisk or a wooden spoon to whip it to incorporate some air and to loosen the texture. Gradually whisk in the sugar. If you add superfine sugar you will achieve a slightly gritty texture, with confectioners' sugar the texture will become much more smooth and creamy, but slightly fondant.

Spoon the mixture into 4 small bowls. Divide the berries between the 4 portions, covering the ricotta. Chill until required, then serve with biscotti or small slices of panettone or pandoro.

Frutta Cotta con la Cannella

Fruit Compote with Cinnamon

This is always present at the breakfast table at my cookery school. It is a good way of using up fruit and is a popular, simple way to start the day. Except the apples and pears, most of the ingredients are optional and dependent upon availability. The secret is to cook everything slowly, to keep the fruit in the largest possible pieces and stir very carefully so as not to effectively turn it all into a purée.

Serves 6–8

1 tumbler orange juice or the freshly squeezed juice of 2–3 oranges
3 apples, peeled and cored
3 pears, peeled and cored
4 or 5 plums or apricots, rinsed and pitted
2 peaches or nectarines, rinsed and pitted
2 small oranges, rinsed and sliced with seeds removed
1 handful pitted dried prunes
1 handful raisins
1 cinnamon stick, about 3in (7.5cm) long
1 clove
generous sprinkling ground allspice
plain yogurt to serve (optional)

Pour enough of the orange juice into a heavy-bottomed saucepan to cover the base, then add the remaining ingredients in layers, finishing off with the rest of the orange juice. Cover the pan tightly, place over a very low heat and allow it to bubble away slowly, slowly, adding a little more orange juice, if required, although the fruit must not swim in liquid. Stir gently once or twice, turning carefully rather than vigorously mixing the ingredients together.

Once the fruit is soft but not about to become soup, turn the whole thing into a large bowl and leave to cool. Gently rearrange the fruit so all the flavors are evenly distributed. Serve at room temperature or slightly chilled, with plain yogurt or on its own.

Uova Strappazzate

Italian Scrambled Eggs

This is the way we've always made scrambled eggs in our house. My boys have been making them like this, as a quick snack, ever since they were able to light the hob. When I was growing up, our eggs would be so fresh and so remarkably delicious that they could be "drunk"—in other words, eaten raw. In Italian, if an egg is really fresh and wonderful, it is called a drinking egg—*uovo da bere*. Needless to say, for this recipe, if the eggs are of drinking standard, then the finished effort is really delectable.

Serves 4
2 tbsp olive oil
8 eggs
dash of milk
salt and freshly ground black pepper

Optional additions can include:
3 tbsp cooked, coarsely chopped mushrooms
4 ripe tomatoes, seeded and roughly chopped
4 cooked Italian sausages, casings removed and roughly chopped
4 slices Parma ham, roughly chopped
1 handful finely chopped mixed fresh herbs

Heat the olive oil in a heavy-bottomed saucepan. While the oil is heating, crack the eggs into a large bowl and add milk, a pinch each of salt and pepper and stir together.

When the oil is sizzling hot, pour in the eggs and raise the heat. Mix together quickly, for 4–5 minutes, allowing the eggs to set and thicken. The effect you are seeking is not that of creamy English scrambled eggs, but a much more rough, lumpy finish—rather like an omelet gone wrong!

Add any or all of the optional additions as soon as the eggs have started to thicken, and mix through as you finish off the cooking.

Ultimate Tomatoes on Toast

Many years ago, when I was first struggling with living in a country that appeared so very different from Italy (and still does!), my best friend Mandy would cook to ease the homesickness. Her dishes included tomatoes on toast. I had by then got used to the apparent English obsession of putting anything and everything on top of a piece of toast—even something called spaghetti, which was anything but pasta as I knew and loved it. The thing about Mandy's tomatoes on toast, which made them so memorable, was that the tomatoes were canned and that they were seasoned, not with salt and pepper as I expected, but with lashings of sugar. I know that the sentiment behind the offering was absolutely genuine, but for me it tasted all wrong, and I have not eaten it since. My tastes are obviously much more attuned to the kind of ingredients I use in this recipe.

Serves 4
12 plum tomatoes, rinsed
4 tbsp extra virgin olive oil
3 garlic cloves, 2 crushed but one left whole
1 handful fresh basil leaves, rinsed and torn, plus extra leaves to garnish
4 thick slices ciabatta, sourdough, casareccio or Pugliese bread—in other words, good-quality, thick bread
sea salt and freshly ground pepper

If the tomatoes have skins that are tough, they will need to be peeled. To do this, cut a small slit in the end of each tomato and put them into a heatproof bowl. Boil the kettle, or a saucepan of water, and pour the boiling water over the tomatoes. Leave them to stand for about one minute, then drain off the water and quickly peel the tomatoes. Squash the peeled tomatoes in your hands lightly to just crush them, and discard any seeds that come loose in the process. Don't fret about the seeds, you can remove them all if you really want to, but otherwise, just relax.

Heat about 3 tablespoons of the oil in a pan with the crushed garlic and fry together very gently until the garlic scents the air. Add the tomatoes and stir together carefully. Cover loosely (by which I mean let the lid rest on the side of the saucepan on the handle of a wooden spoon, so the lid covers only three-quarters of the pan) and simmer for a maximum of 10 minutes, stirring occasionally with care so as not to inadvertently turn the tomatoes into a sauce texture. Season with salt and pepper, stir in the basil and take the pan off the heat.

Meanwhile, toast the bread on both sides, rub one side with the remaining garlic clove and drizzle with the remaining oil. Generously pile the tomatoes on top of the toast. Sometimes I serve these on their own and other times I like to serve them alongside fresh farm eggs fried in olive oil, or with some thick slices of fresh buffalo mozzarella.

Il Porridge d'Inverno
Very Cold Weather Porridge

This is reminiscent of really cold mornings in Tavernelle, when nothing Italian would ever help to warm me, except perhaps for a bowl of very soft polenta, with hot milk poured over it. It is not nearly as appetizing as the rich porridge option that follows. The cold of Tavernelle is possibly the worst cold I have ever experienced. I once spent two days under the covers there, unable to move farther than the bathroom. Though the temperature stayed at −0.4°F (−18°C) for days, hunger eventually drove me to the kitchen. This is always best if you remember to soak the oats and the raisins in the liquid overnight, but whenever I made this for myself or anybody else, I was always so cold in the evenings that I was too focused on getting into bed and warming up to think about any kind of preparation.

Serves 1 very cold person
1 large handful rolled porridge oats
1 handful raisins
pinch of salt
1½ cups (350ml) water
¾–1½ cups (175–350ml) milk
2 tbsp heavy cream
1 tbsp brown sugar
1 shot malt whisky

Put the oats, raisins, and salt in a saucepan and cover with the water and milk, then leave to stand as long as possible, preferably at least one hour.

Place the pan over a low heat and stir gently as the porridge heats and begins to bubble, then continue to stir gently as the porridge becomes more and more creamy and thick.

After about 10 minutes (or longer, it will do no harm), take the pan off the heat and transfer to a warm bowl. Add the cream, sugar, and whisky and prepare to be warmed through and through!

Uova al Prosciutto di Parma
Parma Ham and Eggs

Is this the dish that gave rise to the recipe for *pasta alla carbonara*, as some people would have us believe? The story goes that American GIs kept demanding ham and eggs for breakfast in southern Italy as they traveled northward after World War II. The ever-helpful and gratefully liberated Italians mixed pasta and cooked pancetta with beaten eggs, black pepper, and cheese to make the now-famous sauce (since then so terribly misrepresented by food manufacturers the world over!). I can't help wondering, however, if this might not have been what they actually meant...

Serves 4
1 tbsp unsalted butter
8 eggs
sea salt and freshly ground black pepper
8 thin slices Parma ham
crusty bread, to serve

Warm 4 plates in a low oven.

Melt the butter in a small nonstick skillet. As soon as the butter stops sizzling, break the eggs into the pan, and sprinkle with salt and pepper. Cover and bring to an audible sizzle, then take the pan off the heat, and leave covered for a couple of minutes to finish cooking.

Transfer 2 eggs to each of the warm plates, then return to the oven to keep warm. Return the skillet to a very high heat and as soon as it has resumed its heat, lay the ham in the skillet. Fry very quickly for 1–2 minutes on each side, then arrange on the warmed plates with the eggs, and serve with plenty of crusty bread with which to wipe the plates clean.

La Colazione all'Inglese
An Italian-style Fry-up

My favorite meal is always the last meal that I ate in the company of my sons. Although their likes and dislikes are quite different, this combination of ingredients, and the way in which they are cooked, seems to bring harmony to my little family. We often eat this as a very, very, late breakfast, around 3 p.m.

Serves 3

3 big flat mushrooms, caps and stalks separated
1 garlic glove, crushed to a purée
leaves from 1 small sprig fresh rosemary, finely chopped
5 tbsp olive oil
3 Italian sausages, split in half
12 cherry tomatoes
6 slices thinly sliced pancetta or good-quality bacon
6 eggs or 3 fresh duck eggs
sea salt and freshly ground black pepper
freshly chopped flat-leaf parsley to garnish
bread for toasting
butter

Finely chop the mushroom stalks and blend with the garlic and rosemary. Add one-third of the oil, mix together and season. Use this mixture to brush the mushrooms thoroughly all over and lay them in a ridged griddle pan.

Add the sausages to the griddle pan, skin sides down and griddle for about 5 minutes. Turn the sausages and the mushrooms over, then pour the remaining flavored oil into the top of the mushrooms and continue to cook them. After another 4–5 minutes, add the cherry tomatoes and the pancetta or bacon to the pan, putting the tomatoes in the section of the pan with the most moisture and the meat in the driest area. (If the pan is getting too crowded, use a second pan or just pile everything on top of each other.)

Griddle the pancetta or bacon on each side until crispy round the edges, and cook the cherry tomatoes until they are soft and the skins have split slightly, turning frequently.

In a separate skillet, heat the rest of the oil until just sizzling. Add the eggs, sprinkle with salt and pepper, and then cover and listen for a minute of so until the sizzling intensifies. At this point, you must take the pan off the heat and let the eggs finish cooking under the lid.

While the eggs finish cooking, warm 3 large plates and toast some good bread. Spread the bread thinly with unsalted (preferably Italian) butter. Put the buttered toast at the side of the plate and arrange the rest of the ingredients next to each other on the plate: first the eggs, then the pancetta or bacon, then the mushrooms, the sausages, and the tomatoes. Sprinkle with parsley and serve at once.

Italian Hot Chocolate

This could not be further away from cocoa, a drink that is pleasant enough, but so very different from the luxurious, thick, and sticky chocolate concoction explained below. It is also a completely different concept to that of drinking chocolate, which is just as sweet, but in a completely different kind of way. Besides, this is hot chocolate you can't actually drink, because it is so thick!

Serves 2

7oz (200g) best quality dark chocolate (at least 70% cocoa), broken into pieces
1½ mugs milk
2 tbsp cold water mixed with 1½ tsp cornstarch
1 tbsp superfine sugar
½ tsp vanilla extract
2 heaping tbsp whipped cream (optional)

Melt the chocolate in a bowl set over a saucepan of barely simmering water (do not let the bowl touch the water), stirring until smooth. In a separate pan, heat the milk just until it reaches boiling point, then, off the heat, stir in the cornstarch mixture.

Return the pan to the heat for a few minutes, stirring, then stir in the melted chocolate and whisk together thoroughly. Finally, stir in the sugar and the vanilla. Pour into cups, mugs or small bowls. Drop the whipped cream on top, if using, and serve, with spoons.

La Brioche

Brioche

This rich, eggy, buttery bread is the perfect sort of thing for a truly luxurious breakfast.

Serves 8

¾oz (20g) fresh yeast
¼ cup (50 ml) warm milk
1½lb (750g) white bread flour
2 cups (250g) all-purpose white flour
12 large eggs, beaten, plus 1 extra yolk for glazing
4 tsp sugar
pinch of salt
4 sticks (500g) unsalted butter, softened and broken into small pieces, plus a little extra for the bowl
1 tsp orange flower water

Crumble the yeast into a bowl, stir in the warm milk and set aside until the mixture looks like beer, with a foaming head and a strong smell of active yeast. (See page 30.)

In a separate bowl, mix together both flours, the eggs, sugar, and salt and make a well in the center. Pour in the yeast mixture and stir until a dough forms. Turn out the dough on to the work surface and knead until it is smooth, shiny, and doesn't stick to the surface. It will seem as if you have added many more eggs than you need, but the finished bread will be deliciously buttery and eggy.

Knead in the butter and orange flower water. Shape the dough into a ball. Rub the inside of the bowl with butter, add the dough, and cover with a tea towel. Leave to prove in a warm place for about an hour until it doubles in size.

Knock the dough back and lightly knead, then place in a 1-lb (500-g) floured brioche mold. Re-cover and leave to rise again for about one hour, until it rises to the top of the mold.

Brush the risen dough with the remaining egg yolk and bake in a preheated oven, 325°F, for about 45 minutes until it is golden and sounds hollow on the bottom when you take it out of the mold and tap it. Cool on a wire rack before slicing and serving, or storing.

Chilled Zabaglione

This is one of those marvelously more-ish dishes to serve as part of a brunch. Serve with some hard biscuits, such as *Cantuccini* or *langues de chat* to dunk into the creamy, boozy cream. Zabaglione is one of those legendary desserts that belongs to a time when cooks had a lot more time to dedicate to the preparation of desserts or dishes intended to be made immediately before serving. Served warm, without the mascarpone, in a stemmed glass, this is still one of the best ways to end a meal. This version, however, can be made a couple of hours ahead for stress-free entertaining.

serves 6
6 egg yolks
4 tbsp cold water
6 tbsp Marsala
6 tbsp superfine sugar
4 tbsp very fresh mascarpone cheese, whisked to soften

You need 2 bowls for this dish. The large round bowl for mixing the zabaglione in, preferably copper or glass, should fit comfortably over a saucepan of simmering water without touching the water. Fill a larger, second bowl with ice water and set aside to use in case the eggs start to scramble.

Put all the ingredients into the first bowl and whisk together with a balloon whisk until just blended. Place the bowl over a pan of simmering water and place the pan over a gentle heat—do not let the base of the bowl touch the water. Whisk constantly at an even rhythm, always beating in the same direction, for about 20 minutes until the mixture becomes light, foamy, and pale yellow with the consistency of thick custard. If you undercook the mixture at this point, the liquid will separate from the egg yolks. If the mixture appears to be scrambling, however, take it off the heat immediately, place the bowl in the bowl of ice water and beat hard until it is smooth again. Never allow the water in the saucepan to actually come to a boil.

When the zabaglione is thick and creamy, take it off the heat and transfer it to a cold bowl. Let it cool, whisking occasionally to keep it fluffy. Once cooled, carefully blend in the whisked mascarpone, then transfer into 6 ramekins and chill until required.

Margherita Cake

This is a classic Italian cake recipe and is often present at breakfast, something many of my English friends find a bit odd. But just dunk a slice into a bowlful of real caffè latte or dense Italian Hot Chocolate (see page 21) for a fantastic breakfast treat you will certainly want to return to.

Makes one 10in/25cm cake
6 eggs, separated
6 tbsp superfine sugar
1½ cups (150g) all-purpose white flour, sifted, plus extra for dusting
6 tbsp cornstarch, sifted
1¾ sticks (200g) unsalted butter, melted, plus extra for greasing
½ tbsp grated lemon rind
pinch of salt
confectioners' sugar for dusting

Grease and flour a round 10-in (25-cm) shallow cake pan; set aside.

Put the egg yolks in a bowl, add the sugar and beat until pale yellow. Gradually beat in the flour and then the cornstarch. Beat in the melted butter, the lemon rind, and the salt.

In a separate, spotlessly clean bowl, whisk the egg whites until stiff peaks form, then gently fold into the mixture.

Pour the cake batter into the prepared pan and smooth the surface. Place the pan in a preheated oven, 350°F, and bake for about 40 minutes or until a thin knife inserted into the center comes out clean.

Leave the cake to cool on a wire rack for about 10 minutes in the pan, then turn out of the pan and leave to cool completely. Traditionally, the cake is thickly dusted with confectioners' sugar to serve, leaving a white mustache on many an upper lip. To avoid too much mess, slide the plate on to which the cake will finally be served under the cooling rack, dust the cake with the confectioners' sugar and then transfer the cake to the plate.

Kedgeree all' Italiana

I really love kedgeree, and I have tried very hard to create a version of this good old-fashioned breakfast dish that my Italian family and many friends find remotely palatable, as opposed to simply giving them a strange oddity! (I learned my lesson with porridge!) You can hard-cook the eggs up to a day in advance and keep them in the refrigerator in their shells.

Serves 6

4 fistfuls of long-grain rice
1lb (450g) fresh tuna steak or
10oz (300g) canned tuna in oil, drained
4 hard-cooked eggs, shelled and finely chopped
4 ripe tomatoes, seeded and diced
1 small red onion, finely chopped
10 green olives, pitted and chopped
1 large handful fresh flat-leaf parsley, leaves coarsely chopped
½ lemon
extra virgin olive oil (optional)
sea salt and freshly ground black pepper

Boil the rice in salted water until tender, then drain well, shaking off any excess water.

Meanwhile, if using fresh tuna, heat a skillet or griddle pan over a high heat until smoking. Lay the tuna in the skillet and cook for about 3 minutes on each side, depending on thickness and how well you like it cooked. Remove the tuna from the skillet and leave to rest for a few minutes, then season generously and cut into thin slices.

Place the rice in a large bowl and gently stir in the eggs, tomatoes, onion, olives, and parsley. Season to taste.

Arrange the rice mixture on 6 plates, put tuna slices on top, add a squeeze of lemon and a little olive oil and serve at once. If using canned tuna, however, simply mix it gently into the rice mixture and add a squeeze of lemon and serve.

Luxurious Mushrooms on Toast

This is a very special version of a classic breakfast or supper dish and is unashamedly rich and creamy. If you are anything at all like me, you will only feel less guilty about eating something this fabulously rich if you have actually been out walking and picking the mushrooms yourself!

Serves 6

1lb (500g) mushrooms, wiped and sliced
1 garlic clove, crushed to a smooth purée
½ stick (40g) unsalted butter
3 tbsp brandy or Cognac
1½ cups (350ml) heavy cream
3 tbsp finely chopped fresh flat-leaf parsley
sea salt and freshly ground black pepper
Brioche (see page 21) or good-quality toast, buttered, to serve

Prepare the mushrooms first. Fry the garlic and the butter together gently for 3–4 minutes, then add the mushrooms. If there are too many mushrooms for the pan fear not! You must simply wait for the first batch of mushrooms to lose their moisture and cook down slightly, thus making space in the pan for another batch. When the mushrooms have reabsorbed all their moisture, they are cooked.

Add the brandy and set light to it, then wait for the flames to go out. Now add seasoning and the cream. Stir gently until everything is heated through again and bubbling hot. Sprinkle with a little parsley and tip out onto thoroughly buttered brioche or toasted bread. Serve at once, before all the cream and the buttery mushroom juices are too far soaked into the bread. This is wonderful on its own, or alongside some thinly sliced Parma ham.

Salame Frittata

Salami Frittata

A frittata is a flat Italian omelet, made using all sorts of different ingredients, from cooked vegetables to cheese. I often put out one or two different flavors of frittata as part of a brunch. You can make this version using either cubed or sliced pancetta, thinly sliced Parma ham or even mortadella. The choice of salami is important, as it completely changes the taste of the finished dish. Bear in mind that the orange/red color found in many different kinds of salami is a sure indication there is plenty of chili in the meat mixture, and salami from Tuscany often contains fennel seeds, so always taste before you buy.

Serves 4

4oz (115g) salami of your choice, casing removed, if necessary, and cubed
1 tbsp olive oil
5 organic eggs
4 tbsp freshly grated Parmesan cheese
sea salt and freshly ground black pepper

Fry the salami gently in a heavy-bottomed skillet (about 6–7in/15–18cm) over high heat for about 5 minutes or until it gives off its fat. Add a tablespoon of olive oil to the rendered fat and swirl it around so the base and side of the skillet are coated.

Beat the eggs in a bowl with a pinch each of salt and pepper and the Parmesan. Pour the eggs over the salami, shaking the skillet to spread out the eggs. Turn down the heat and leave the frittata to cook for about 5 minutes until the base is golden brown and set—use a spatula to lift the edge and peep underneath.

Carefully slide the frittata on to a plate. Put the skillet over the frittata, upside down, then invert the plate and skillet. Return the skillet to the heat and continue cooking for about 4 minutes until the base is set. Slide on to a flat platter to serve either hot or cold, cut into wedges.

Omelette con la Marmellata

Plum (or other) Conserve Omelet

I am not a great one for skiing, but I do like going on skiing holidays with friends and cooking for them! This is a skiing holiday breakfast favorite, and tastes hugely better than it sounds. The quality of the conserve is essential. I have suggested you use my favorite kind, which is a tart, low sugar plum conserve made with "susine"—a type of semi-wild plum that grew profusely in our garden at home in Italy.

Serves 1

2 eggs
1 tbsp milk
1 tsp unsalted butter
2½ tbsp sour plum jam
a little confectioners' sugar
sea salt and freshly ground black pepper

Break the eggs into a bowl and add the milk and salt and pepper to taste. Whisk together until everything is just combined.

Melt the butter in a small omelet or nonstick skillet, swirl it around the base and sides and wait for it to stop moving (pause) in between sizzling and starting to brown. When the butter pauses, pour the eggs in. Tip the skillet around and draw the cooked edges of the omelet into the center of the pan. Keep doing this, moving the pan around as necessary. As soon as the omelet is more or less set, put the jam in the center, fold the omelet in half and tip it onto a plate. It should take less than a minute from when the egg hits the pan to when it reaches the plate—it must never brown!

Dust the folded omelet with confectioners' sugar and serve at once.

Panino con la Frittata

Vegetable Frittata Sandwich

The quantity of vegetable to egg varies enormously, depending upon which kind of vegetable you are using. The basic rule is that there has to be enough beaten egg to hold the whole thing together, but there must be enough vegetable content for the vegetable to form the main part of the finished dish. I tend to use about two-thirds cooked vegetable to one-third beaten eggs. Be very careful not to add too much cheese, as this can make the frittata stick to the base of the pan, and thus make it impossible to turn the frittata over successfully. The amount of time it takes to cook a frittata will depend on how thick it is, and what kind of pan you are using. My very favorite frittata is with cooked artichokes, which given the amount of time it takes to just clean and trim the artichokes, requires a great deal of time and care, but the finished dish is very special indeed.

Serves 4–6

12oz (375g) Swiss chard, spinach, zucchini, onions, or any other chosen vegetable, boiled, steamed, or sautéed, then carefully drained to remove all excess liquid

6 eggs, beaten

¼ cup (25g) freshly grated Parmesan cheese

4 tbsp olive oil

sea salt and freshly ground black pepper

6 crusty rolls to serve

Whichever vegetable you choose to put into the frittata, it must be as dry as possible for the finished frittata to retain the texture that makes it easy to slice into wedges. In the case of green, leafy vegetables, such as chard or spinach, this means squeezing the water out of the cooked leaves before chopping finely; all other vegetables just need to be very thoroughly drained of any liquid.

Mix the hot or cold vegetable into the beaten eggs, then add in the Parmesan and salt and pepper to taste. Heat the oil in a heavy-bottomed, 6–7in (15–18cm) skillet. When it is very hot, pour in the egg mixture, shaking the pan to spread out the ingredients, pulling the liquid egg into the center as you work. Cook until the underside is browned and firm.

Carefully slide the frittata onto a plate. Put the skillet over the frittata, upside down, then invert the plate and skillet. Return to the heat and continue cooking for about 4 minutes until the base is set.

Slide out onto a flat platter and leave to cool. When it is time to eat, slice the frittata into 6 wedges. Slice 6 crusty rolls in half and slip a wedge of frittata inside each. Press the rolls closed firmly, so some of the juices and moisture seep into the bread, and serve at once.

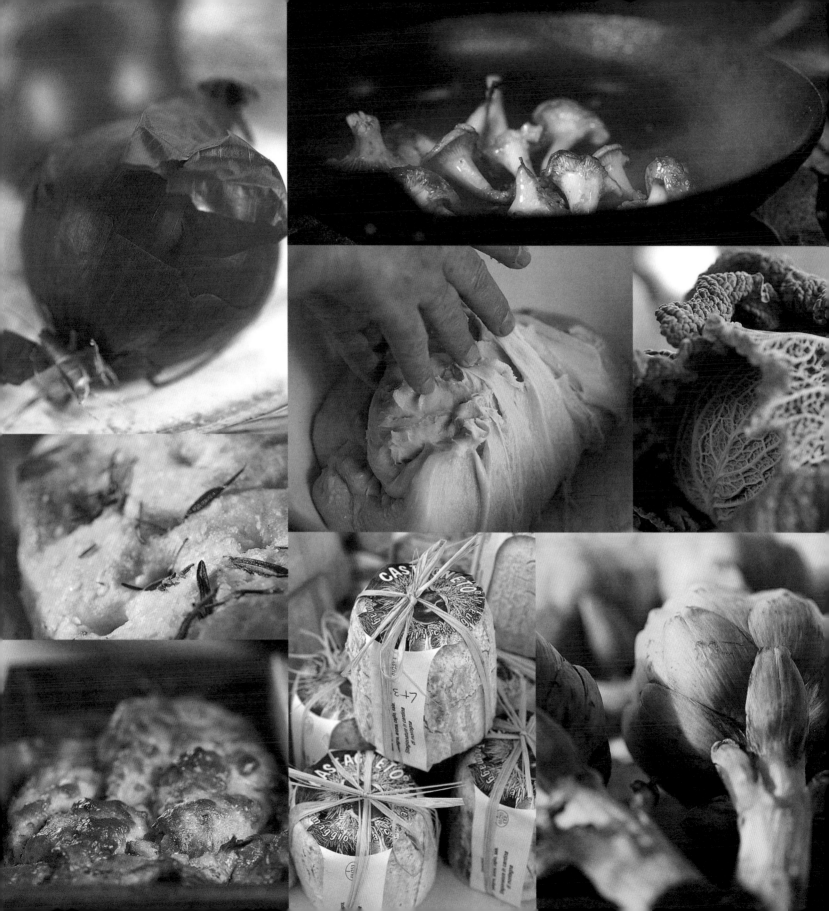

2 slow snacks for sharing

Between running a restaurant and a cookery school, writing, consulting, and teaching, my life is nothing if not irregular in terms of mealtimes. My household consists of my two lovely sons and one daughter-in-law, all of whom appear to be permanently hungry and happy to eat whenever food is available rather than at any accepted set times. This made the recipe testing of what follows very easy, as they were more than happy to eat and offer up constructive criticism at any time of the day or night! For me, cooking food from scratch is never a chore, as I enjoy every moment, from the shopping to the washing up—all are part of the rituals of family life. Even though my children are now fully grown men, they will always have an Italian mamma in the kitchen! These are any time of the day recipes, perfect for those occasions that call for something to nibble on, such as warm pumpkin chips with a fennel seed pesto, or a slice of farinata wrapped around a slice or two of salami.

Focaccia Ripiena

Stuffed Focaccia

I know a restaurant in Italy that is the ultimate focaccia establishment. The focaccia there is just right—not too dense and cake-like in texture, oily enough and with just enough salt. The forty or so fillings are varied and interesting, and you are allowed your own combinations. There are soft, sweet, roasted bell peppers; fragrant, fresh vongole; every kind of salami, as well as speck and prosciutto; creamy, slightly sour cheese mixed with braised peas and even soft, pure white mozzarella and ripe, soft tomatoes. Your slice of focaccia is split open and filled with whatever you have chosen, then shut and put into a hot oven to heat through. I have had many glorious meals under the pine trees of this marvelous establishment—two of my favorite fillings follow.

Makes 1 large loaf (or 3 medium-sized loaves or 6 single portions)

1oz (25g) fresh yeast
1¼ cups (300ml) warm water
pinch of granulated sugar
3¼ cups (400g) white bread flour
coarse sea salt
2–3 tsp olive oil

Mix the yeast and water together, then add the sugar and about 2 tablespoons of the flour. Put the yeast mixture somewhere warm to activate for about 30 minutes. (The airing closet, or next to the boiler are all excellent places; failing that, you can hold the bowl against your own body until the froth begins to appear on the surface. No matter how many times I make bread dough of any kind, this coming to life of the yeast is always like a little tiny miracle—just as amazing every time as the first time you see it happen.)

When the yeast mixture is fizzing gently and has formed something of a head, like on a glass of ginger beer, you know there is life once again in the yeast and you can now add it to the flour. Tip the remaining flour on to the work surface and make a well in the center. Pour the yeast mixture into the well, then knead it energetically into the flour, adding a little more water as required. Add the salt and the oil and knead hard for about 10 minutes until the dough is soft, elastic, and slightly shiny. Shape the dough into a ball and put it into a large floured bowl, cover with plastic wrap (oil the underside of the wrap lightly to prevent it sticking against the rising dough) and leave somewhere warm to rise again for about 2 hours or until it has doubled in size.

Knock back the dough, tip it out onto your work surface and need lightly. Using well-oiled hands, shape the dough into a flat round (or pull it into pieces and shape into 3 medium-sized or 6 single rounds), flattening it between your palms to the desired thickness (bearing in mind it will rise again and thus will become even thicker). Place the dough on a well-greased baking sheet and leave to rise again for another hour or until double in volume. Use your oiled fingertips to make indentations all over the surface of the risen foccacia, then drizzle with the olive oil and sprinkle with salt. Place in a preheated oven, 425°F, and bake for 10–12 minutes or until the top is golden and crisp and the focaccia moves freely on the baking sheet. Slide it off the baking sheet to cool until required. You can eat the focaccia as it is, or use one of the ideas for a filling shown opposite.

Fillings:

You can put almost anything you like inside a slice of focaccia, from slices of Parma ham with a couple of sliced figs, to fresh ricotta with salami or pan-fried mushrooms. Try one of the following ideas (each makes enough to fill 1 large, 3 medium-sized, or 6 single-portion foccacias):

Sweet Bell Pepper Filling

Fry 1 chopped garlic clove in 5 tbsp extra virgin olive oil just until it turns brown. Use a slotted spoon to remove and discard the garlic. Add 10oz (300g) chopped onion and continue frying until just soft, but not colored. Stir in 1lb (500g) seeded, cored and chopped red or yellow bell peppers (or a mixture) and 10oz (300g) chopped tomatoes. Add ½ glass dry white wine and salt and pepper to taste, then cover the pan and simmer over low heat for about an hour, stirring frequently. Use hot or at room temperature.

Clam Filling

I love clams. They have to be one of the most delicious and precious of all the treasures of the sea. This filling idea also works perfectly with fresh mussels.

Thoroughly clean 3lb (1.5kg) fresh clams by leaving them overnight in several changes of cold, salted water to remove all traces of sand or mud. Discard any clams with cracked shells or open shells that don't snap shut when tapped.

Heat 3–4 tbsp oil in a pan large enough to hold all the clams, with 5 chopped garlic cloves, 4 coarsely chopped fresh parsley sprigs, and 1 bay leaf and fry for about 3 minutes. Stir in the drained clams. Cover and leave the clams to simmer over a low heat, shaking the pan occasionally, for about 5 minutes until all are open. Discard any clams that remain closed.

Remove the pan from the heat and strain the juices into a bowl. Remove the clams from the shells, then stir them into just enough of the reserved cooking juices to keep them moist. Reheat them gently and use to fill the focaccia.

Panzanella al Basilico

Fried Breadsticks with Basil

Longer ago than I want to remember, I used to travel for well over an hour on a hot summer's afternoon to go and sample the best *panzanella* in the world at a remote shack in a field, down a dirt track. I couldn't possibly find it again now, but then, surrounded by friends and caught up in the moment, it mattered not one bit where we were going or how we were going to get home again! Once again, this is a recipe using poor, simple ingredients, but the end result is captivating. Not to be confused with the Tuscan bread salad of the same name, this kind of snack can also be found at most beachside bars in northern Tuscany.

Makes about 20
1oz (25g) fresh yeast
1¼ cups (300ml) warm water
pinch of granulated sugar
3¼ cups (400g) white bread flour
1 handful fresh basil leaves, rinsed and dried
2–3 tsp olive oil, plus extra for deep-frying
pinch or two of sea salt, to taste
freshly sliced Parma ham to serve

Mix the yeast and water together, then add the sugar and about 2 tablespoons of the flour. Put the yeast mixture somewhere warm to activate for about 30 minutes.

When the yeast mixture is fizzing gently, tip all the remaining flour on to the work surface and make a well in the center. Pour the yeast mixture into the well, then knead it energetically into the flour, adding a little more water as required. Add the salt and the oil and knead hard for about 10 minutes until the dough is soft, elastic, and slightly shiny. Shape the dough into a ball and put it into a large floured bowl, cover with plastic wrap (oil the underside of the wrap lightly to prevent it sticking against the rising dough) and leave somewhere warm to rise again for about 2 hours or until the dough has doubled in size.

When you want to turn your dough into panzanella, turn it out onto the work surface, knock it back and give it a quick knead. Pull the dough apart into long, sausage-shaped sections with well-oiled hands. Push 1, 2, or more basil leaves into each piece of dough.

Meanwhile, heat enough olive oil for deep-frying in a heavy-bottomed saucepan until it is sizzling (around 375°F/190°C). Working in batches, if necessary, drop the dough strips into the hot oil and fry quickly, turning them frequently to make sure they puff up and become golden and crisp. Drain thoroughly on paper towels and sprinkle with a little salt. Serve at once, with a platter of freshly sliced Parma ham.

Farinata
Thin Chickpea Slices

When you first make *farinata*, known as *socca* in Nice, you will be a little alarmed at quite how liquid the batter is, but fear not as it will pull together into a smooth pancake as it bakes. This is the poorest of foods, just finely ground chickpeas, water, oil, and salt and pepper—and yet it manages to be one of the most more-ish and delicious things to eat. Try not to eat it all before serving it to your guests! I think these are wonderful with stracchino cheese, or with salami, or just on their own—but always best warm from the oven.

Serves 6
2 cups (300g) chickpea flour
4–5 cups (1.35 litres) water
4 tbsp olive oil
sea salt and freshly ground black pepper

Put the chickpea flour in a bowl with the water and mix together thoroughly. Add 2 tablespoons of the oil and salt and pepper to taste and beat until a batter forms. Leave the mixture to stand for about an hour or even overnight—the longer the better.

Use the remaining oil to grease a wide, shallow, rimmed, baking sheet and then pour in the mixture. Place in a preheated oven, 400°F, and bake for 30 minutes or until crisp on the outside and still soft in the middle. You should end up with a wide sheet of farinata no more than 2–3cm (¾–1¼in) thick. Serve warm from the oven, though it is also quite good cold.

Crostini di Polenta con Porri e Pancetta
Leek and Pancetta Polenta Crostini

This is a great way to eat polenta, even for those who swear they can't stand the stuff! Very tasty, these make wonderful little snacks to nibble while sipping a good red wine, and are easily passed around a party. Cheese- and flour-free, these are also great for those guests who have various food allergies.

Serves 4
1 large leek, chopped and rinsed
2½oz (65g) pancetta, cubed
4oz (115g) cooked spinach,
Swiss chard, or cabbage, drained and
finely chopped
3 cups (800ml) water
1 cup (150g) polenta
extra virgin olive oil for brushing
sea salt and freshly ground black pepper

Fry the leek gently with the pancetta until the leek is soft and the pancetta browned and crispy. Stir in the spinach.

In a separate pan, bring the water to a boil with a pinch of salt. Stir in the polenta, reduce the heat, and boil slowly, stirring continuously, for about 45 minutes until thick. Take the pan off the heat, then stir in the leek, pancetta and spinach mixture. Stir together thoroughly and add seasoning to taste.

Tip out the polenta on to a lightly oiled rimmed baking sheet, spread it into a thin layer with a wet or greased metal spatula and allow to stand until cold.

Heat the broiler until hot or a griddle pan until it is smoking hot. Cut the cool polenta into diamonds or squares, and brush lightly with extra virgin olive oil on both sides. Broil the polenta on both sides for about 2 minutes, or until crisp on the outside and hot all the way through. Serve hot.

Sfogliata con Porri e Olive Nere

Leek and Black Olive Tart

A lovely, crumbly, flaky tart with plenty of flavor and texture. It is easy enough to make, and you could, if you prefer, make your own pastry.

Serves 4

½ stick (50g) unsalted butter, plus extra for greasing the dish

8oz (250g) ready-made puff pastry, thawed if frozen

6 leeks, thinly sliced and rinsed, with any tough green sections discarded

3½ tbsp all-purpose white flour

1½ cups (350ml) milk

3 tbsp freshly grated Parmesan cheese

12 black olives, pitted

6 paper-thin slices of speck or prosciutto

sea salt and freshly ground black pepper

Grease a medium-sized shallow ovenproof serving dish generously with butter. Roll out the pastry until it is slightly larger than the dish then press it into the dish, trimming off any excess pastry. Prick with a fork in several places across the base. Put in the refrigerator until needed. Preheat the oven to 400°F.

Melt the remaining butter in a saucepan. Add the leeks and fry them for about 10 minutes or until soft. Sprinkle the flour over the leeks and gently stir together, then gradually pour over the milk, stirring constantly. Simmer, still stirring, for 4 minutes. Season to taste, and then stir in the Parmesan and the olives.

Lay the speck slices on top of the puff pastry in the dish, then add the filling.

Transfer the *sfogliata* to the oven and bake for about 30 minutes, until the pastry is risen and golden. Allow to cool slightly before serving.

Mixed Vegetable Bruschetta

I was in the Siena area recently and discovered bruschetta as I had not known it before, with all kinds of vegetable toppings. My favorites were the cavolo nero and the radicchio versions, both of which had a delicious bitterness that was perfect with the dense bread and the luscious oil. Here are my adaptations.

Makes 8 slices
8 slices ciabatta or coarse, crusty Tuscan style bread
1 garlic clove
2 tbsp olive oil
sea salt and freshly ground black pepper

For the radicchio topping (for 4 slices):
3 tbsp olive oil
2 heads radicchio, quartered, well rinsed and finely shredded
1 tbsp balsamic vinegar

For the cavolo nero topping (for 4 slices):
3 tbsp olive oil
2 garlic cloves, finely chopped
2 canned anchovy fillets, chopped
½ large head cavolo nero, or one whole smaller head, rinsed, dried and coarsely shredded

Toast the bread until golden on both sides. Rub each slice with the garlic and drizzle lightly with olive oil. You can do this after you prepare the toppings, or before and just hope the toast doesn't get eaten in the meantime!

To make the radicchio topping, heat the oil in a skillet for a few minutes, then add the radicchio. Stir the radicchio and oil together, season and douse with a little cold water to encourage the radicchio to wilt. Cover and leave the radicchio to cook over a low heat for 5–10 minutes, until softened. Spoon the hot radicchio on top of 4 slices of the garlic-flavored toast and drizzle with the balsamic. Serve at once.

To make the cavolo nero topping, heat the the oil in a skillet for a few minutes with the garlic and the anchovy fillets, stirring until the anchovies dissolve. Add the cavolo nero and stir together, adding a little cold water to help the leaves to soften and wilt. Cover and leave the cavolo nero to cook over a low heat for 5–10 minutes, until softened. Spoon the hot cavolo nero on top of the bread and serve at once.

Ham and Cheese Bruschetta

You can adapt either of the previous bruschetta recipes by combining the vegetables with ham and cheese—I like to use fontina, but you can use any cheese. Take care to get it right: the bread must be toasted to the right point, the cheese must be melted just so and the ham has to be crisp but not dry.

Serves 4
4 slices ciabatta or coarse, crusty Tuscan-style bread
½ garlic clove
4 tbsp extra virgin olive oil
4 slices fontina cheese, about the same size as the bread slices and 1cm (½in) thick
4 slices prosciutto or speck, large enough to completely cover the cheese

Toast the bread until golden on both sides. Rub each slice with the garlic and drizzle lightly with olive oil.

Lay a slice of fontina on top of each slice of toast, big enough to almost cover the entire surface of the bread, then slip it back under the broiler to just soften the cheese. Remove the bread from the heat again and lay a slice of prosciutto or speck on top of the melting cheese, covering the cheese entirely. Broil again until the fat at the edges of the ham begin to color and crisp up, curling in the process. Serve at once.

Zucca Fritta col Pesto di Finocchietto

Pumpkin or Butternut Squash Chips with Fennel Seed Pesto

The pumpkin is an underrated vegetable which deserves to be used much more widely. This is a great favorite snack of mine which looks as good as it tastes!

Serves 6

10oz (300g) pumpkin or butternut squash, seeded but not skinned

all-purpose white flour

1½ cups (75g) soft white breadcrumbs

1 tsp fennel seeds, lightly crushed

1 sprig fresh fennel leaves

1 garlic clove

sea salt and freshly ground black pepper

sunflower oil for deep frying

2 tbsp cider vinegar, or white wine vinegar

Cut the pumpkin into irregular shaped slices 3 or 4mm (less than ¼in) thick. Bring a large saucepan of salted water to the boil and drop the slices into the water for 1–2 minutes, then remove with a slotted spoon and leave to dry on a folded, dry tea towel. Dust lightly on both sides with flour.

Meanwhile, whiz the breadcrumbs, fennel seeds, fennel leaves and garlic together in a food processor for a minute or so, then season to taste.

Heat the oil until it reaches 350–375°F/180–190°C, or a cube of bread browns in 30 seconds. Add the dry pumpkin slices in batches and deep-fry until golden brown, then remove with a slotted spoon and drain on paper towels.

Pile the chips on a platter, sprinkling with the breadcrumb mixture and finally drizzle over the vinegar. Serve at once.

Fett'unta

Garlic Bread

I think this is the ultimate garlic bread, made in the traditional way, as they have made it in Tuscany for time immemorial. Naturally, to be a complete traditionalist, you'd use unsalted Tuscan bread for this recipe, but I have found it hard to find outside of a very specific area around Florence and Siena. You really do have to use the very best deep-green Tuscan olive oil, however, with plenty of peppery bite and the flavor of newly cut grass for this to taste as good as it can. This is absolutely wonderful on its own, but also delicious with thinly sliced prosciutto, salami, or mortadella, or when used to line a bowl of soup.

Makes 2 slices

2 thumb-thick slices of good Tuscan or country bread

2 garlic cloves, cut in half

plenty of really good Tuscan olive oil

sea salt

Toast the bread lightly until golden on both sides. Rub the bread thoroughly with the garlic, then drench the bread with oil so it is slightly dripping and softened. Sprinkle with salt—and that's it! Add a topping, if you, want, but it is still pretty good on its own.

Riso al Salto

Flash in the Pan Rice

The skill of this dish, which has to be one of the most perfect ways of using up leftover risotto, is in having the skillet hot enough to start with. You must be brave enough to use one made of cast iron or stainless steel, and get it hot and oily so the rice turns out like a perfect, flat, thin pancake. The most important ingredient, to begin with, is the leftover risotto. Traditionally, this should be Milanese risotto (saffron-flavored) or mushroom risotto, but, in reality, any will work as long as it is not a fish or shellfish risotto. This makes a perfect pre-dinner nibble.

Serves 4

12oz (350g), about 2 cups, cooked, leftover risotto (see page 45, but remember that 1¼lb (600g) raw rice will make about 2lb (1kg) cooked risotto, so use about a third of the quantities given there)
small amount of water, or chicken or vegetable stock
4 tbsp olive or sunflower oil
sea salt and freshly ground black pepper (optional)

Mix up the leftover risotto, which will have become thick and sticky, with a little water or stock, just to loosen it up. If necessary, add a little seasoning.

Heat a cast iron or stainless-steel skillet until it is very hot, then add the oil and swirl around. Tip in the risotto. The secret now is to take the skillet off the heat and flatten the risotto thoroughly and evenly, using a palette knife, the back of a spoon or whatever implement you have in your armory that fits the bill best! Work quickly so the skillet doesn't cool down too fast—you are trying to get the pancake super crispy, but without letting it stick!

Once the risotto is crisp and golden on the base, loosen it all around and turn it over quickly, either by flipping it (this being the *salto*—or the "jump"). Or make life easier for yourself by inverting it on to a large plate, lightly oiling the skillet, and then gently sliding it back in. Cook the other side over medium to high heat for another 5 minutes or so, then slide the rice pancake onto a plate. Cut into slices and serve at once.

Uova al Forno

Eggs *en Cocotte*

This just has to be the best brunch food! Make sure the eggs are super fresh. This is also one of those great do-it-yourself dishes—get your guests to prepare the eggs in the ramekins with their chosen added ingredients, then the eggs can be quickly baked and served to order. The basic recipe could not be simpler and can be adapted to any number of guests.

For each portion
small amount of unsalted butter, plus extra for the ramekin
1 tbsp light cream
1 egg
sea salt and freshly ground black pepper
toast or good crusty bread to serve

Butter a ramekin, then spoon in the cream. Break the egg carefully on top of the cream. Drop a tiny bit of butter on top of the yolk, and sprinkle the egg with salt and pepper.

Place the ramekin in a baking pan with enough water to come two-thirds of the way up the side of the ramekin. Place in a preheated oven, 400°F, and bake for about 5 minutes, until the egg has just set. Serve the egg with toast or a couple of slices of good crusty bread.

Variations:

Eggs *en Cocotte* with Shrimp for 4
Boil 8 raw shrimp in salted water until they turn pink, then drain and remove the shells when cool enough to handle. Prepare 4 ramekins as above and add one shrimp to each. Break an egg on top of each shrimp, then add 1 tablespoon light cream and another shrimp to each ramekin. Sprinkle with chopped fresh parsley, chopped garlic and salt and pepper to taste. Bake as above for about 5 minutes, until set.

Eggs *en Cocotte* with Peas for 4
Prepare 4 ramekins as above. Melt about ¼ stick butter in a pan, add 5 tablespoons cooked peas and 3oz (75g), about ½ cup, diced cooked ham and fry for about 5 minutes. Season with salt and pepper to taste.

Divide the pea and ham mixture between the ramekins, then break an egg into each ramekin. Sprinkle each with chopped fresh parsley and ½ tablespoon light cream. Bake as above for about 5 minutes, until set.

Eggs *en Cocotte* with Anchovies for 4
Prepare 4 ramekins as above. Place one drained canned anchovy fillet in each ramekin, then break an egg over each. Add a second anchovy fillet and 1 tablespoon light cream on top of each egg. Grind over some pepper and add a final dot of butter to each Bake as above for about 5 minutes, until set.

Red Onion Loaf

This very soft, very tasty loaf is delicious as an hors d'oeuvre or appetizer, or as part of a picnic. What is especially delicious about this loaf is that it stays wonderfully moist.

Serves 6

2oz (50g), about 2–3 slices, stale white bread
scant ½ cup (100ml) milk
1 tbsp extra virgin olive oil
7oz (200g) speck or other smoked cured ham, thickly sliced and cubed
2 large red onions, coarsely chopped
6 fresh chives, chopped
6 fresh sage leaves, chopped
2 eggs
2 tbsp all-purpose white flour
½ cup (50g) freshly grated Parmesan cheese
1½ tsp baking powder
sea salt and freshly ground black pepper
unsalted butter for greasing
2 tbsp dried white breadcrumbs

Tear up the bread, put it in a bowl, pour over the milk, and leave to stand until required. Meanwhile, put the oil, speck, or other ham, onions, and herbs in a skillet and fry over medium heat, stirring often, until the onions are soft. Remove the skillet from the heat and set aside.

Strain the bread from the milk, reserving the milk.

Crack the eggs into a bowl and beat them thoroughly, then add the drained bread, the flour, Parmesan, and baking powder, then stir in the onion and speck mixture, and season with salt and pepper.

Thoroughly butter a 1¾-pint (1-liter) loaf pan. Sprinkle the base and sides with the dried breadcrumbs, then spoon in the onion mixture and level the surface. Place in a preheated oven, 350°F, for 40–45 minutes until a knife inserted into the center comes out clean. Remove from the oven and leave to rest for about 10 minutes before turning out the onion loaf and slicing thinly. Serve at once, with a cheese platter or some cured meats, such as prosciutto or bresaola.

Taleggio and Pear Savory Tart

I really love pears, and believe they are much under-used! I make them into salads, sauces, desserts, cakes and savory tarts, rather like this one.

Serves 4

8oz (250g) ready-made puff pastry, thawed if frozen
3 tbsp dry breadcrumbs or cracker crumbs
3 ripe pears, peeled and thinly sliced
8oz (250g) taleggio cheese, derinded and diced
scant ½ cup (100ml) light cream
pinch ground cinnamon
sea salt and freshly ground black pepper

Generously grease a 10½-in (26-cm) pie pan with a removeable base and place on a baking sheet. Use the puff pastry to line the tart tin and press the edges to the sides firmly with the back of a fork. Scatter the crumbs all over the base of the pastry. Preheat the oven to 425ºF.

Arrange the pear slices over the crumbs. Put the cheese and the cream in a bowl over a pan of simmering water and stir until the cheese has melted completely. Pour this mixture over the pears, then sprinkle with the cinnamon and salt and pepper.

Place the tart in the preheated oven, and bake for about 30 minutes, until set. Remove from the oven and leave to cool for about 5 minutes, then carefully remove from the pan and serve just warm.

Palline di Mozzarella
Fried Mozzarella Balls

These really are fabulous, and must be served with a dipping sauce—I usually opt for a fiery arrabbiata with a basic sweet tomato sauce as an alternative, though I can also recommend a bowl of fresh green pesto for dunking. These are so good that you'll find yourself making more before too long!

Serves 4
6 tbsp dried breadcrumbs
3 mozzarella (not buffalo) balls,
about 3½oz (80–100g) each, drained
and chopped
3 large eggs
10 fresh sage leaves
leaves from 1 sprig fresh rosemary
1 garlic clove, chopped
¼ cup (40g) freshly grated Parmesan cheese
3 tbsp all-purpose white flour
sunflower oil for deep-frying
sea salt and freshly ground black pepper

For the arrabbiata sauce:
4 garlic cloves, finely chopped
1–4 dried red chilis (depending upon how
hot you want the sauce!)
4 tbsp extra virgin olive oil
13oz (400g) canned chopped tomatoes,
drained if necessary
1 tsp chopped fresh parsley

For the sweet tomato sauce:
4 tbsp extra virgin olive oil
1 onion, very finely chopped
1 large celery stalk, strings removed and
finely chopped
1 large carrot, peeled and finely chopped
13oz (400g) fresh or canned tomatoes,
or passata (crushed tomatoes)
a few celery leaves or herb leaves, finely
chopped (optional)

Put half the breadcrumbs into the food processor with the mozzarella chunks. Add one of the eggs, the herbs, garlic, Parmesan, and seasoning to taste. Whiz until you have created a mixture that is fairly lumpy and reasonably dry. Roll the mixture into about 10 walnut-sized balls. Put the flour on a plate, beat the remaining 2 eggs in a shallow dish and place the remaining 3 tablespoons of breadcrumbs on another plate.

Roll the cheese balls in the flour, then in the beaten eggs, and finally in the breadcrumbs. Arrange the cheese balls on a freezerproof tray and freeze for at least 30 minutes. Meanwhile, make the sauces. To make the arrabbiata sauce, fry the garlic and chilis in the olive oil, stirring, until slightly blackened, then remove them from the pan and discard. Add the tomatoes with seasoning to taste and bring to a boil, stirring. Reduce the heat and simmer for 20 minutes, stirring occasionally. Remove from the heat, adjust the seasoning, if necessary, and stir in the parsley. Transfer to a bowl and set aside.

To make the sweet tomato sauce, pour the oil into a heavy-bottomed saucepan, add all the vegetables, except the tomatoes, and fry over a low heat for about 5–8 minutes until soft and the onion becomes transparent. Only at this point, stir in the tomatoes. Cover and leave to simmer for about 30 minutes, stirring regularly. Season to taste. If you want to add celery leaves or herbs, stir them in now when the sauce has finished cooking.

When you are ready to fry the mozzarella balls, heat enough oil for deep-frying until it reaches 350–375°F/180–190°C, or until a cube of bread browns in 30 seconds. Working in batches, add the mozzarella balls and deep-fry for about 5 minutes, until golden and crisp all round. Remove with a slotted spoon and drain well on paper towels. Serve hot with the sauces for dipping.

Suppli alla Scamorza
Suppli with Scamorza

Suppli are little rice fritters that are very popular in Rome. There are few things that are more delicious than crisp *suppli* with a gooey cheese filling. The type of cheese used for the filling can be mozzarella, fontina, Emmenthal or, as in this case, smoked scamorza. Scamorza is mozzarella that has been allowed to dry and has then been lightly smoked to preserve it and to add a very different flavor. This labor-intensive snack is worth every delicious mouthful. First, make the risotto as detailed below and allow it to cool. Or simply use leftover risotto, about 1lb (500g) and preferably reasonably plain so that the scamorza flavor can really dominate.

Makes about 20

13oz (400g) smoked scamorza, cubed

2 tbsp chopped fresh flat-leaf parsley

3 tbsp cooked mushrooms, zucchini or spinach, finely chopped

4 eggs, beaten

3 tbsp all-purpose white flour

4 tbsp dried white breadcrumbs

sea salt and freshly ground black pepper

For the risotto:

1 onion, finely chopped

¾ stick (75g) unsalted butter

1¼lb (600g) risotto rice

about 6 cups (1.5 litres) best-quality chicken or meat stock, or very flavorsome vegetable stock, kept hot

6–7 tbsp freshly grated Parmesan cheese

If you don't have leftover risotto, begin by making a fresh pot, but be sure to allow enough time for it to cool before you plan to fry the *suppli*. To do this, fry the onion in half the butter for about 10 minutes over very low heat or until the onion is soft but not colored. Stir in the rice and toast the grains thoroughly on all sides, stirring, so they are opaque but not colored. Add a ladle of hot stock and stir it in, letting the rice absorb the liquid and all its flavor, stirring constantly. Continue adding all the stock, ladleful by ladleful, until the rice is almost completely soft and creamy.

Stir in the cheese and the rest of the butter, then taste and adjust seasoning. Cover the pan for about 5 minutes, then remove the lid and leave to cool before making the *suppli*. (Or, to serve hot, leave to stand for about 3 minutes, then transfer to a platter.)

When the rice is completely cool, stir in the smoked scamorza, parsley, half the eggs, the cooked vegetables, and seasoning to taste. Mix all the ingredients together well.

Lightly flour your hands and roll the rice mixture into fat sausages, then roll them lightly in the flour, then the remaining beaten egg, and finally the dried breadcrumbs. Arrange on an oiled baking sheet, brush with more olive oil very gently.

Place the *suppli* in a preheated oven, 375°F, and bake for about 10 minutes until crisp and golden brown. Alternatively, to be more traditional, deep fry in hot sunflower oil, 350–375°F/180–190°C, or until a cube of bread browns in 30 seconds, until golden and crispy on the outside. Work in batches, if necessary, and drain well on paper towels before serving hot.

3 long, lazy lunches

I have always somehow preferred lunch to dinner.
Perhaps because I generally prefer cooking in the
morning, and sitting down to a very long and leisurely meal
that can stretch into the late afternoon feels perfect to me.
My training as a chef means I find it hard to leave the kitchen
messy after cooking, and to wake up to a debris-cluttered
kitchen the morning after a dinner has never seemed much
fun. Better by far to clear up at the end of a very long lunch,
then collapse into bed! In this chapter you will find dishes
that to my mind suit the middle of the daytime slot, but like
all the recipes throughout the book, they are, of course,
completely interchangeable to suit your own requirements.
Just add some really good bread, some delicious wine,
appreciative guests, and comfortable chairs…

Il Minestrone

Real Minestrone

There are two ways of approaching the creation of this great classic soup. You can, for example, use up any number of leftover vegetables that are looking a little tired, or you can use deliciously fresh vegetables that you have selected especially. The difference is remarkable. Whether you use dried or canned beans makes little difference to the finished dish, as there are lots of other tastes going on at the same time, but if you use fresh borlotti, you will definitely be able to tell!

Serves 4–6

7oz (200g) dried (1½ cups), or fresh borlotti beans, shelled if fresh, or the equivalent tinned borlotti beans, drained and rinsed
4 tbsp olive oil
2 large onions, coarsely chopped
1 handful fresh flat-leaf parsley, chopped
1 leek, finely chopped and rinsed
3 carrots, scraped and diced
2 zucchini, diced
10oz (300g) green leaf vegetable, such as spinach, cabbage, Swiss chard, lettuce leaves, or turnip tops, trimmed as necessary and chopped
2 potatoes, peeled and diced
4 cups (1 liter) chicken or vegetable stock, plus extra for simmering the beans in, if desired
7oz (200g), or 2 cups, short stubby pasta or 1 cup long-grain rice
sea salt and freshly ground black pepper

To serve:
olive oil
freshly grated Parmesan cheese

First, attend to the beans. Cover them in cold water and soak them overnight, then drain and rinse them. Return them to the saucepan with fresh water to cover, bring to a boil and boil hard for 5 minutes. Drain the beans again, return to the pan, cover with fresh water (or stock) and return to a boil, then reduce the heat and leave to simmer until they are tender—the exact time will depend on how old they are. Do not add salt to the water until the beans are tender, as this will cause the skin to shrivel and harden. Do not drain the beans when they are tender, because you will use the cooking water in the soup.

Next, fry the onion in the olive oil for about 5 minutes, stirring occasionally. Add the parsley, then all the vegetables, adding them gradually in batches so they wilt down and create space as you go along. Stir together and cook for a further 5 minutes.

Pour in the beans and all their water. Add the stock and bring to a boil, then reduce the heat and simmer for about 1 hour, stirring frequently and topping up with water or stock, until the vegetables are tender. Be sure to add more water if necessary to maintain enough liquid to cook the vegetables and to be able to call it a soup and not a stew.

Add the pasta or rice once the vegetables are thoroughly cooked. Serve hot as soon as the pasta or rice is tender, or leave to cool and serve at room temperature, or even—as in some parts of Lombardy—chilled.

Variations:

To make this soup with fresh borlotti beans, you will need 1lb (500g) in the pods. Shell the beans, then put them in a pan with water to cover, bring to a boil and boil hard for 5 minutes. Drain the beans, cover with fresh water (or stock), and return to a boil, then reduce the heat and leave to simmer until they are tender. Add the beans and their cooking liquid to the soup, as above.

To use canned beans, drain and rinse 13oz (400g) beans and add them to the soup at the same time as the pasta or rice to heat through.

Minestra di Patate con i Gamberi
Creamy Potato Soup with Crisp Shrimp

This is a luxury version of a potato soup, though it can also be made using squash for a different, sweeter flavor. For a lighter version, simply boil or steam the shrimp, then peel and add to the soup.

Serves 4

For the soup:
3 large shallots, sliced
4 tbsp extra virgin olive oil
1lb (500g) floury potatoes, such as Yukon Gold, peeled and diced
2½ cups (600ml) vegetable stock
¾ cup (200ml) heavy cream
1lb (500g) raw shelled shrimp, headless, deveined, and rinsed
sunflower oil for deep-frying
sea salt and freshly ground black pepper

For the batter:
¼ cup (40g) all-purpose white flour
5–6 tbsp water
1 egg white, chilled

Fry the shallots in the oil for about 4 minutes, then add the potatoes and stir together for a couple of minutes. Pour in the stock and season to taste. Cover the soup and leave to simmer for about 20 minutes, or until the potatoes are completely falling apart. Pour the soup into a food processor or blender and whiz until smooth, adding a little vegetable stock if too thick. Return the soup to the rinsed-out saucepan and season to taste, keeping it warm over very low heat.

Meanwhile, to make the batter, whisk the flour and water together with a pinch of salt to form a thick paste with the texture of melted ice cream. In a separate bowl, whisk the egg white until it holds a stiff peak, then gently fold this into the flour paste.

Heat enough oil for deep-frying in a heavy-bottomed saucepan or a deep-fat fryer until it reaches 350–375°F/180–190°C, or until a cube of bread browns in 30 seconds. Dry the shrimp thoroughly. Working in batches to avoid over-crowding the pan, dip them into the batter to coat them thoroughly, letting the excess batter drip back into the bowl. Drop them into the hot oil and fry until crisp and golden brown. Drain thoroughly on paper towels.

Bring the soup back to a boil, then take the pan off the heat and whisk in the heavy cream. Pour the soup into 4 heated soup bowls and drop an even number of the hot, crisp shrimp in the center of each bowl of soup. Sprinkle with a little pepper and serve.

Pasta and Chickpeas

This is an ancient recipe. In fact, some say it is the earliest recorded pasta recipe, going right back to the time of the Roman legionnaires, who apparently made a version of this dish at their encampments. If you don't like the flavor of anchovies or chilis, leave them out and just stick with the oil and garlic. This is a very chunky, thick, substantial soup, which improves greatly if made the previous day and then reheated at the last moment. You can, of course, make it meaty by adding some chopped smoked pancetta to the garlic in the very first part of the method, or by adding a ham bone to the simmering chickpeas.

Serves 6

2¼ cups (300g) dried chickpeas, or
1¼lb (625g) canned chickpeas, drained and rinsed
9 garlic cloves, crushed to a purée
9 tbsp olive oil
up to 6 cups (1.5 liters) water
2 sprigs fresh rosemary, about 2in (5cm) each
6 salted anchovy fillets, boned, rinsed and very finely chopped
½ tsp chopped dried red chilis
2 tbsp tomato paste
2½ cups (300g) cannolicchi, ave marie, or other short, stubby pasta
sea salt and freshly ground black pepper

To garnish:
1–3 tbsp olive oil
4 twists of the peppermill

Put the dried chickpeas into a large bowl and cover generously with cold water, then leave to soak overnight. The next day, drain and rinse them thoroughly. Return them to the saucepan with plenty of cold water to cover, bring to a boil and boil hard for 5 minutes, then drain and rinse again. Return the chickpeas to the heat, covered by fresh water and bring to a boil again, then reduce the heat and simmer gently until tender—the exact time will depend on how old they are. Remove the pan from the heat and set aside for the moment; do not drain.

In a separate large, deep pan, fry half the garlic with 3 tablespoons of the oil for about 5 minutes. Add the softened or canned chickpeas and stir together thoroughly. Pour in the water, including the water in which the chickpeas were boiled if you have used dried chickpeas, and add the rosemary. Stir in salt and pepper to taste, cover the pan, and leave to simmer for about 30 minutes or until the chickpeas are slightly mushy.

Meanwhile, put the remaining garlic and oil in a separate small pan with the anchovy fillets, chilis and tomato paste. Fry together very gently, stirring frequently. When the mixture is perfectly amalgamated, remove from the heat but keep warm.

Add the pasta to the chickpeas and stir together. Allow the soup to bubble for long enough to cook the pasta, then take it off the heat and drizzle the top with the anchovy mixture to add extra heat and flavor. You can omit the topping, of course, but it is absolutely delicious! Drizzle over the olive oil and sprinkle over the pepper, then serve.

Zuppa di Pesce
Fish Soup

This is the easiest recipe for making a really tasty fish soup. You can add mussels, shrimp and all manner of other fish or shellfish if you wish, although the basic recipe here calls only for filleted white fish, which makes it really easy to eat. The bread soaks up all the flavors and juices of the fish and is eaten at the end, once all the fish has been consumed.

Serves 6

about 4lb (2kg) various filleted white fish,
such as cod, angelfish, haddock, plaice
and so on
½ cup (125ml) olive oil
6 garlic cloves, one left whole, the others
finely chopped
1 dried red chili
6 tbsp chopped fresh flat-leaf parsley
3 handfuls cherry tomatoes, sliced in half
1 large glass dry white wine
about 3½ cups (900ml) fish stock
12 thin slices ciabatta or other crusty
bread, toasted
sea salt and freshly ground black pepper
2 tbsp extra virgin olive oil to serve

Prepare all the fish first. Trim it carefully, then wash and dry it all.

Heat the oil in a deep saucepan over medium heat with the chopped garlic, chili, 4 tablespoons of the parsley and the tomatoes and fry for about 5 minutes, stirring occasionally. Add all the fish and stir gently so as not to break it up. Pour over the wine and the fish stock and season with salt and pepper. Cover the pan tightly and simmer very gently for about 10 minutes.

Meanwhile, rub the toast with the whole garlic clove and use the bread to line a large wide serving bowl. Pour the hot fish and all the liquid all over the bread, drizzle with a little olive oil, sprinkle with the remaining 2 tablespoons of parsley and serve at once.

Pasta e Fagioli
Pasta and Beans

There are many recipes for this soup, as each region of Italy seems to have their own version. Basically, the recipe is always more or less the same, with a few variations, such as the addition of other vegetables, herbs, pancetta, chili, or sometimes a different kind of bean. This is different from Real Minestrone (see page 48), insofar as it is really about the beans and the pasta, rather than all the vegetables.

Serves 4

10oz/1½ cups (300g) dried cannellini and/or borlotti beans

3oz (75g) fatty pancetta or prosciutto (optional)

1 onion, chopped

1 large carrot, peeled and chopped

1 large celery stalk, chopped

3 tbsp olive oil

2 tbsp tomato paste, diluted in 4 tbsp boiling water

4 cups (1 liter) meat or vegetable stock

1 heaping cup (150g) small soup pasta

sea salt and freshly ground black pepper

extra virgin olive oil for drizzling

freshly grated Parmesan cheese for sprinkling

Put the dried beans into a large bowl and cover generously with cold water, then leave to soak overnight. The next day, drain and rinse them thoroughly. Put the beans in a saucepan, cover with plenty of fresh cold water, bring to a boil and boil hard for 5 minutes, then drain and rinse again. Return the beans to the heat with fresh water to cover and return to a boil, then reduce the heat, and simmer for 40 minutes or until they are almost tender—the exact time will depend on how old they are. Drain the beans and set aside.

Having prepared the beans, fry the pancetta, onion, carrot, and celery in the olive oil for about 5–8 minutes until the vegetables are all soft. Stir in the tomato paste and drained beans and stir thoroughly. Add the stock and simmer slowly for about 30 minutes until the beans are almost falling apart.

Stir in the pasta and continue cooking until it is tender. Season to taste and serve warm, drizzled with a little extra virgin olive oil, and with a light sprinkling of Parmesan.

Variations:

To make this soup with fresh cannelloni and/or borlotti beans, you will need 1½lb (750g) in the pods. Shell the beans, then put them in a pan with water to cover, bring to a boil and boil hard for 5 minutes. Drain the beans, cover with fresh water (or stock), and return to a boil, then reduce the heat and leave to simmer until they are tender. Add the beans and their cooking liquid to the soup, as above.

To use canned beans, drain and rinse 13oz (400g) beans and add them to the soup at the same time as the pasta or rice to heat through.

Savory Cheesecake with Radicchio

Robiola is a very creamy cheese from Piemonte, used a great deal in cooking throughout the north of Italy. If you can't find any, choose a full-flavored cream cheese instead.

Serves 8

about 8 slices (300g) dry, stale whole-wheat toast

1 stick (100g) unsalted butter, melted, plus a little unmelted butter for greasing the pan

4 eggs

1¼lb (600g) robiola cheese

½ cup (100ml) milk

1 cup (100g) freshly grated Parmesan cheese

generous grating of fresh nutmeg

3 tbsp extra virgin olive oil

1 dried red chili

1 sprig fresh rosemary

1 large head radicchio, washed and left wet

sea salt and freshly ground black pepper

Whiz the toast in a food processor or blender until reduced to fine crumbs, then stir in the melted butter and one egg to make a smooth paste. Grease and line a 9½-in (24-cm) springform cake pan with baking parchment, then cover the base with the crumb paste, and set aside.

Beat the robiola with the milk, Parmesan, remaining eggs, nutmeg, and salt and pepper. Put this mixture into the prepared cake pan and smooth the surface. Place in a preheated oven, 350°F, and bake for 30 minutes.

Meanwhile, heat the oil in a skillet with the chili and the rosemary and fry for about 5 minutes, stirring occasionally. Remove the rosemary and the chili and discard, then stir the wet radicchio into the flavored oil and cook for about 6 minutes, turning frequently, until wilted. Remove the pan from the heat, and when the radicchio leaves are cool pull them apart. Take the cake out of the oven and let it cool for a few minutes, then remove the cake from the pan and arrange the wilted radicchio leaves over the top. Although this can be eaten cold, it is best served while still warm.

Beef Pizzaiola

The name of the dish indicates that it is similar to pizza, but, in fact, it is only the sauce that is served with thin slices of meat. The ratio of sauce to meat is deliberately unbalanced, so if you like, you can save some of the sauce to toss with pasta. The brief "cooking" method ensures the meat remains tender. There should be plenty of oregano and garlic so the flavors shine through. Just make sure the oregano is pungent before adding it to the sauce. Pizzaiolas are also delicious served with garlic-flavored mashed potatoes.

Serves 6

2 garlic cloves, chopped

4 tbsp olive oil

8oz (250g) canned chopped tomatoes or passata (crushed tomatoes)

1 heaping tsp dried oregano

6 thinly sliced beef steaks, about 6oz (180g) each—sirloin works best

sea salt and freshly ground black pepper

plenty of crusty bread to serve

Gently fry the garlic with the olive oil in the largest skillet or sauté pan you have for about 5 minutes, until it is soft, then pour in the tomatoes. Stir and simmer, uncovered, for about 10 minutes, then add the oregano and season with salt and pepper.

While the sauce simmers, put the steaks in between sheets of parchment paper and carefully batter them with a meat mallet or rolling pin until they are really thin. Trim off all fat and gristle. Add the steaks to the tomato sauce, cover the pan, and turn off the heat, then leave to stand for about 6 minutes so the meat just cooks through and remains tender.

Remove the steaks from the pan and arrange on a platter. Cover with the sauce and serve at once with crusty bread to mop up all the sauce.

Fresh Tomato Sauce

There are so many different versions of tomato sauce throughout the length and breadth of Italy, one could devote a whole book to this subject alone. This, however, is the most simple, basic sauce, to which any number of other herbs or flavors can be added, and which changes completely in character depending upon whether you add butter or oil at the end. If the sauce is too liquid, just boil it fast in a wide pan until it reduces. As well as using this sauce for pasta, it can be used as the basis for all sorts of savory dishes: pizza or crostini topping, Pizzaiola (see page 55), soups, and so on.

Makes about 2 cups (500ml)—enough for 6 portions of pasta
2lb (1kg) fresh tomatoes, skinned, seeded, and quartered
1 small onion, quartered
1 carrot, peeled and quartered
1 celery stalk, quartered
1 large sprig fresh flat-leaf parsley
7 leaves fresh basil
3 tbsp olive oil
1 tbsp unsalted butter, or 2 tbsp extra virgin olive oil
sea salt and freshly ground black pepper

Put all the ingredients, except the butter or extra virgin olive oil and salt and pepper, into a large saucepan. Cover and bring to a boil, stirring occasionally, then reduce the heat and simmer for 30 minutes. Uncover the pan and continue to simmer for a further 20 minutes or so, until most of the liquid has evaporated.

Remove the pan from the heat and push the sauce through a food mill or sieve, or whiz in a food processor, until smooth. Season with salt and pepper to taste and reheat to serve.

If you want to enrich the flavor and texture, add either the butter or extra virgin olive oil to the sauce as soon as it has been heated through. Do this off the heat, because the idea is not to cook the butter or oil, but just to stir it through.

Basic Pizza Dough

This is the most simple version of pizza dough, which can also be used to make focaccia. If left to rise overnight, it will make a basic sour dough.

Makes 6 single portion pizzas or focaccia
3¼ cups (400g) white bread flour
1oz (25g) fresh yeast
¾ cup (200ml) warm water
salt
2 or 3 tsp olive oil

Mix the yeast and water together and add about 2 tablespoons of the flour. Put the yeast mixture in a lightly floured bowl and place it somewhere warm to rise for about 30 minutes. Tip the remaining flour on to the work top.

Once it has risen, knead the yeast mixture thoroughly, and then knead it into the rest of the flour, adding a little more water as required. Add the salt and the oil and knead energetically together for about 10 minutes. Transfer this mixture to a large floured bowl and return to the warm place to rise again for about an hour or until doubled in size. Use as required.

La Sfoglia
Basic Pasta Dough

Some purists say that fresh pasta is best when made entirely by hand, without using a machine at all. Although this requires more of an effort, the result will be quite amazingly good, albeit always slightly thicker than if you had rolled and cut the pasta with a machine rather than with a rolling pin and a knife. I think the important thing about fresh pasta is being able to taste the love and effort which has gone into making it in every delicious bite.

Makes about 500g (1lb)

1lb/3½ cups (500g) all-purpose white flour, or half fine semolina and half all-purpose white flour

5 large eggs

Making the dough:
Put the flour in a mound on the work surface and plunge your fist into the center to make a hollow. Break the eggs into a bowl and beat them together thoroughly with a fork. Pour the beaten eggs into the hollow, then begin to knead them roughly into the flour with your fingertips, then use your hands to knead everything together. Remember, you are not making pastry—this is not the moment for a delicate approach! Knead the flour together until you have a really smooth, pliable ball of dough.

Leave the dough to rest under a clean cloth or in plastic wrap for 20 minutes. This will relax the gluten and make the dough more manageable. Do not refrigerate at this point.

Rolling out pasta dough by hand:
Flour the work surface and rolling pin lightly, and roll out the dough as thinly as possible with a strong, long rolling pin. Continue to roll it over and over again until your dough is really elastic, smooth, and shiny. It should cool considerably as you work it. When it is ready, the sheet of dough will feel exactly like a brand new, wrung out, damp chamois leather. Proceed to cut, shape, and/or fill the pasta immediately as instructed in your recipe, covering any rolled-out pasta you aren't using with a slightly damp, clean tea towel to prevent it drying out as you work.

Rolling out pasta dough by machine:
If you use a pasta machine, leave the dough to rest as above, then break off a piece about the size of a small fist. Always rewrap the pasta you are not using to prevent it drying out. Flatten the piece you have broken off with your hands and push it through the widest setting on your pasta machine. Fold it in half and repeat. Do this 3 more times. Move the machine down to the next setting and repeat rolling out the dough 3 more times. Continue in this way, changing the setting after every 3 rolls until you hear the pasta snap loudly as it is going between the rollers. At this point you can forget about folding it in half each time, as the snap indicates that the surface tension of the pasta is now correct. Continue to wind it through the rollers to the last or penultimate setting on the machine, depending on how fine you want it to be.

Proceed to cut, shape, and/or fill the pasta immediately as instructed in your recipe, covering the rolled out pasta with a slightly damp clean tea towel to prevent it drying out as you work.

Parmigiana di Carciofi
Globe Artichokes with Parmesan Cheese

The labor of love that goes into the preparation of this sumptuously delicious dish is all in the preparation of the artichokes. If you are not used to cleaning and preparing them, you'll be stunned at the mountain of waste that ensues! You really do need 40, maybe even more, and they are time consuming indeed when it comes to stripping them. I think it's worth every moment though! Your hands might blacken as you work with this iron-rich vegetable, so keep a halved lemon or two around with which to cleanse your fingers.

Serves 8
40 large globe artichokes
1lb (500g) fresh mozzarella cheese, drained and thinly sliced
1¾ cups (200g) freshly grated Parmesan cheese
sea salt and freshly ground black pepper

For the Tomato Sauce:
4lb (2kg) fresh tomatoes, skinned, seeded and quartered
2 small onions, quartered
2 carrots, peeled and quartered
2 celery stalks, quartered
2 large sprigs fresh flat-leaf parsley
12 leaves fresh basil
4 tbsp olive oil

First, prepare the tomato sauce. Put the tomatoes, onions, carrots, celery, and parsley in a large saucepan. Add 3 tablepoons of cold water to prevent the vegetables from catching, cover the pan and bring to a boil, then reduce the heat and simmer for 30 minutes. Remove the lid and continue to simmer for about 20 minutes, until most of the liquid has evaporated. Remove the pan from the heat and push the sauce through a food mill or sieve, or whiz in a food processor, until smooth. Season with salt and pepper to taste, and then stir in the basil and the olive oil, and set aside until required.

Next, prepare the artichokes carefully, one at a time. Remove all the outer, hard leaves [1] and trim away the stalk. Cut off all the sharp tips with a pair of scissors. Cut the artichoke horizontally across the base [2] and carefully scrape out the furry choke [3]: you should end up with just the flat base. Drop this into a basin of cold water with a couple of sliced lemons to prevent it oxidizing and set aside until required.

Bring a large pan of salted water to a boil, add the artichokes and boil slowly until they are just tender when pierced with a fork or knife. Drain well and set aside.

Spoon a little tomato sauce across the bottom of a large ovenproof serving dish. Arrange a layer of artichokes over the tomato sauce, cover with half the mozzarella and Parmesan, then cover with the remaining sauce, another layer of artichokes and, finally, the last of the cheeses. Leave the dish to stand for about 10 minutes or put in the refrigerator for up to 2 hours, until needed.

Place the dish in a preheated oven, 375°F, and bake for about 30 minutes or until bubbling hot and brown on the surface. Allow to stand for about 5 minutes before serving. This is also delicious served at room temperature.

Pumpkin and Zucchini Molds

These are like little savory puddings, which taste quite sweet thanks to the pumpkin. To cut the sweetness, I like to spoon over a few spoonfuls of a simple sauce of Gorgonzola, slowly melted into a little milk over a low heat and gently stirred until smooth.

Serves 6

butter for greasing the ramekins
breadcrumbs for lining the ramekins
1lb (500g) pumpkin peeled and seeded
3 zucchini, diced
1 large onion, chopped
1 cup (250ml) chicken or vegetable stock
4 tsp mild curry powder
1½ pinches chili powder
3 pinches freshly grated nutmeg
1 handful fresh basil leaves, rinsed
and dried
3 eggs, separated
2 tbsp extra virgin olive oil
sea salt and freshly ground black pepper

Butter 6 x ½-cup volume (125-ml) ramekins and line them with breadcrumbs; set aside. Cut 10oz (300g) of the pumpkin into small cubes; set aside the remaining pumpkin.

Put the diced pumpkin in one saucepan and the zucchini in another. Add one-quarter of the onion to each pan, and divide the stock between the 2 pans, keeping about one-third of the stock in reserve. Flavor each pan with 2 teaspoons curry powder, half the chili powder, half the grated nutmeg, and salt and pepper to taste. Place the 2 pans on the heat and simmer gently until the onion, zucchini and pumpkin are all softened and cooked through. Divide the basil leaves between the 2 pans and stir.

Whiz the pumpkin and the zucchini separately in the blender, being sure to rinse out and dry the bowl in between to keep the colors pure.

Beat the egg yolks and mix half into the pumpkin and half into the zucchini. Whisk the egg whites until stiff peaks form, then fold half into the pumpkin purée and half into the zucchini purée.

Divide the zucchini mixture between the ramekins and smooth the surfaces. Spoon the pumpkin purée into the ramekins, on top of the zucchini purée, and smooth the tops again. Put the filled ramekins in a roasting pan containing enough water to come two-thirds of the way up the sides.

Put the roasting pan in a preheated oven, 325°F, and bake for about 30 minutes until the purées are set. Meanwhile, put the remaining onion, the remaining stock, the rest of the spices, and salt and pepper in a pan and simmer for about 20–30 minutes until completely softened. Transfer the pumpkin to a blender and whiz until smooth, then blend in the olive oil.

Remove the ramekins from the oven and invert them on to warm plates, surround with the hot pumpkin cream and serve at once.

Gnocchi di Farina di Castagne al Gorgonzola

Chestnut Gnocchi with Gorgonzola

In the part of Tuscany where I come from, sweet chestnut flour is very widely used and much prized. Indeed, in the not so distant past, this was the only flour widely available in the more remote, poorer mountain areas. Many of the old mills can still be seen, nestling by the side of a rushing stream in the middle of dense chestnut woods.

Serves 4
2½ cups (1 pint) milk
2 cups (500ml) water
¾ cup (100g) fine semolina
1½ cups (200g) chestnut flour
2 egg yolks
¾ cup (75g) freshly grated Parmesan cheese
7oz (200g) Gorgonzola cheese
½ stick (50g) unsalted butter
sea salt and freshly ground black pepper

Put 2 cups (500ml) of the milk, the water, and a pinch of salt into a large saucepan over high heat and bring to a boil. Sprinkle in the semolina with one hand so it falls like rain into the water, whisking constantly with the other hand to prevent lumps forming. Sift in the chestnut flour, whisking constantly, and continue to simmer for about 10 minutes, stirring, until a thick paste forms. Take the mixture off the heat and allow the semolina to cool for about 5 minutes.

Whisk the egg yolks into the semolina, one at a time. Tip the mixture out onto a work surface, dampened with cold water to prevent sticking, and spread out with a wet metal spatula and your wet hands to an overall thickness of about ½in (1cm); leave to cool completely and set.

Using a 2-in (5-cm) cookie cutter, cut the chestnut semolina into circles. Arrange a layer of scraps from the cut-out semolina on the base of 4 buttered flameproof serving dishes, then equally divide the semolina circles between the dishes.

Melt the Gorgonzola in a small pan over a low heat with the remaining ½ cup (100ml) milk and the butter, stirring constantly. Pour one-quarter of this sauce over each of the 4 dishes of gnocchi, then sprinkle with the Parmesan. Put the dishes under a preheated broiler and leave for about 3 minutes until the tops are golden brown and bubbling. Serve the gnocchi at once.

Gnocchi alla Romana al Salmone

Semolina Gnocchi with Smoked Salmon

One of the most comforting of all the dishes in the Italian repertoire has to be semolina gnocchi. I find something very safe and reassuring about the texture and flavor. By adding a little smoked salmon and a handful of snipped chives, the simple dish is elevated to new levels of of sophistication.

Serves 6
4 cups (1 liter) milk
1¾ cups (250g) fine or medium semolina
2 egg yolks
7oz (200g) smoked salmon, chopped
1 bunch of fresh chives, snipped
1 cup (100g) freshly grated Parmesan cheese
1 stick (100g) unsalted butter
sea salt and freshly ground black pepper

For the béchamel sauce:
½ stick (50g) unsalted butter
¼ cup (40g) all-purpose white flour
2 cups (500ml) milk

First make the béchamel sauce. Melt the butter until foaming, then quickly stir in all the flour. Stir over the heat until a soft paste forms, then pour in all the milk and whisk until smooth. Simmer gently, stirring, until thickened, and season with salt and pepper. Cover the surface with a little cold water, or a piece of plastic wrap, to prevent a skin from forming; set aside until required.

Next, move on to the semolina gnocchi. Bring the milk to a boil in a large saucepan. Sprinkle in the semolina with one hand so it falls like rain into the water, whisking constantly with the other hand to prevent lumps forming. Continue whisking until the mixture begins to thicken, then use a wooden spoon to stir constantly for about 10 minutes as the mixture thickens. You know it is ready when it begins to come away from the side and the base of the pan and forms a rounded, soft ball.

Remove the pan from the heat, then stir in the egg yolks one at a time, the chives, smoked salmon, and ½ stick (50g) of the butter, stirring until the butter melts and is absorbed. Season with salt and pepper.

Lightly dampen your work surface with cold water and tip the semolina on to it. Use a wet metal spatula to spread out until it is about ½in (1cm) thick. Using a 2-in (5-cm) cookie cutter or an up-turned tumbler, cut all the semolina into even-sized circles.

Use some of the remaining butter to grease a shallow, ovenproof serving dish. Arrange a layer of scraps from the cut-out semolina circles on the base of the dish. Cover with the béchamel sauce and a few dots of butter. Add a sprinkling of Parmesan, then a layer of slightly overlapping semolina circles. Repeat the layering until all the ingredients have been used, except a small amount of the butter. Melt the remaining butter and trickle it over the top. Place the dish in a preheated oven, 400°F, and bake for about 15 minutes. Serve hot.

Calzone con Salsa di Pomodoro
Calzone with Tomato Sauce

The word *calzoni* means trousers, as these puffed-up, folded pizzas are supposed to look like a folded pair of pantaloons! Using the basic pizza dough recipe (see page 56), you can make four small or two large calzone. Treat the list of filling ingredients as a guideline and vary it according to your own tastes. For a party, make smaller, individual calzone and deep-fry them in sunflower oil.

Makes 2 large or 4 small calzone
1 quantity Basic Pizza Dough (see page 56)
sea salt and freshly ground black pepper
2 tbsp extra virgin olive oil
2 garlic cloves, finely chopped
13oz (400g) chopped plum tomatoes
2 tbsp chopped fresh flat-leaf parsley
extra virgin olive oil for greasing and brushing

Filling ingredients:
4 tbsp ricotta cheese
6 slices salami, rind removed, if necessary, and coarsely chopped
4 sun-dried tomatoes in olive oil, drained and chopped
2 tsp chopped fresh flat-leaf parsley

Make the pizza dough as instructed on page 56, and set aside, covered, to rise until doubled in volume.

To make the sauce, gently fry the garlic in the oil for about 5 minutes, until the garlic is soft, but not brown or the sauce will taste very bitter. Stir in the tomatoes and bring to a boil, stirring. Reduce the heat, cover, and simmer for about 15 minutes, then stir in the parsley and season to taste. Remove the sauce from the heat and use as required. This will keep for a couple of days in the refrigerator.

Turn out the dough on to a lightly floured surface and knead for a few moments. Divide it into 2 or 4 equal-sized pieces. Working with one piece of dough at a time, and keeping the surface lightly floured, roll it out into a thin circle.

Lay the dough circles on a lightly greased baking sheet and spread 1 tablespoon ricotta over each, keeping it to one side and to the center of the circle so you can fold the calzoni in half and seal it effectively. (You might need to use 2 baking sheets, depending on their size and the size of your oven.) Sprinkle the salami, the sun-dried tomato, and the parsley on top of the ricotta, then drizzle with a little olive oil and season lightly with salt and pepper. Fold each calzoni in half and press all along the open edge with the back of a fork to seal securely.

Place the baking sheet in a preheated oven, 400°F, and bake for about 15 minutes, until puffed and golden brown. Meanwhile, reheat the tomato sauce. Serve straight from the oven with the tomato sauce offered separately.

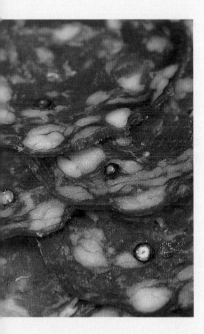

Torta Salata di Polenta con Funghi e Pancetta
Polenta Cake with Mushroom and Pancetta Filing

This is a seriously filling dish that requires only a very simple green salad to follow, and maybe a refreshing fruit salad. Polenta makes you feel very full immediately after eating it, but it is quickly digested, so later in the afternoon you could serve a little something like a cake or some homemade cookies, and I think your guests will probably be ready for it! The ideal scenario is to serve this after a long mushroom hunt so everybody feels hungry, and there is nothing quite like the triumph of finding your own wild mushrooms and using them immediately. In the absence of freshly gathered wild funghi, however, use 1½lb (750g) good-quality, tasty cultivated mushrooms. You can also always add a handful of reconstituted dried porcini for extra flavor. I have yet to find a quick-cook polenta that is any good, so I always like to use the traditional 50-minutes variety … but you may think differently!

Serves 6

1lb (500g) coarse or fine polenta
5½–6 pints (2.75–3 liters) cold water
½ cup (50g) freshly grated Parmesan cheese
1lb (500g) wild mushrooms, such as porcini or similar, cleaned, trimmed, and roughly chopped
8oz (250g) chanterelles or similar exotic mushrooms, cleaned, trimmed, and roughly chopped
4 tbsp olive oil, plus extra for greasing
2 garlic cloves, chopped
2 tbsp chopped fresh flat-leaf parsley
1 sprig fresh thyme
7oz (200g) Italian cooked ham (prosciutto cotto), thickly diced
7oz (200g) fontina cheese, cubed
sea salt and freshly ground black pepper
Tomato Sauce (see page 56) or Parsley Mushrooms (see page 81) to serve

First make the polenta. Bring the water to a boil in a wide, heavy-bottomed, preferably copper, saucepan over a high heat. Sprinkle in the polenta with one hand so it falls like rain into the water, whisking constantly with the other hand to prevent lumps forming (this is easiest to do with a friend).

When all the polenta has been whisked into the water, reduce the heat to medium-low, add the Parmesan and seasoning to taste, and then begin to stir constantly with a strong, long-handled wooden spoon until the polenta comes away from the side of the pan. This will take 40–50 minutes and requires patience, energy, and a strong elbow. Remove the pan from the heat and allow the polenta to cool a little before using two-thirds of it to completely line an oiled 8-in (20-cm) round deep spring-form cake pan with a removable base. Spread the remaining one-third of the polenta on a lightly oiled board into a circle roughly the size of the cake pan to make the lid. Set aside the lined pan and the polenta for the lid.

Meanwhile, cook the mushrooms. Gently fry the garlic in the oil for about 5 minutes, until the garlic is tender, but not browned. Add the mushrooms and continue frying until they are soft. Stir in the parsley and thyme and salt and pepper to taste. Remove the pan from the heat and set aside to cool.

Remove the thyme sprig and spoon one-third of the mushroom filling into the polenta-lined cake pan, then add a layer of ham and fontina. Continue layering until all the ingredients are used. Position the reserved circle of polenta on top and seal the edge by pressing the polenta into position with your fingers.

Place the cake pan on a baking sheet in a preheated oven, 400°F, and bake for 20–30 minutes. Take the polenta cake out of the oven and leave to rest for 5 minutes, then turn out of the pan and slice into wedges. Serve with a simple tomato sauce or with yet more mushrooms.

Brustengo di Patate e Cavolo

Potato and Cabbage *Brustengo*

I guess this is the nearest thing to the very English bubble-and-squeak that you will find in Italy, made very tasty with the addition of garlic, bacon fat, and olive oil. This is really good alongside a dish of Italian sausages stewed with tomato sauce and borlotti beans, on a cold winter's day after some strenuous outdoor activity, such as snow shoveling!

Serves 6

1 very large onion, thinly sliced
½ cup (125ml) extra virgin olive oil
1 small savoy cabbage, shredded
1¼ cups (300ml) vegetable stock
750g (1½lb) floury potatoes, such as Yukon Gold, unpeeled
3 garlic cloves, thinly sliced
2oz (50g) pancetta, chopped
sea salt and freshly ground black pepper

Fry the onion in half the oil until golden. Add the cabbage and mix together, then pour over the stock, cover the pan and bring to a boil. Reduce the heat and leave to cook for about 20 minutes, stirring occasionally and adding more stock if required, until soft. Make sure the cabbage is reasonably dry, not sitting in liquid, draining it, if necessary, then turn it into a bowl; set aside.

Meanwhile, in a separate pan, boil the potatoes in plenty of salted water for about 30 minutes from the time the water starts boiling, until very soft. Drain the potatoes and, when cool enough to handle, peel them and mash with a fork. Stir the potatoes into the cabbage

In a nonstick skillet, heat the remaining oil with the garlic and pancetta and fry for about 3 minutes, or until the garlic is smelling strong. Tip the potato and cabbage mixture into the hot, oily pan. Press down to flatten evenly, then fry for about 5 minutes on one side until crisp and golden. Turn over as though you were turning a frittata (see page 26) to cook the other side until equally crispy and golden. Cut into wedges and serve at once, piping hot.

Patate Farcite

Stuffed Potatoes

This is my take on the old jacket potato option. I like to serve these with a lovely green leaf, fresh herb and avocado salad, dressed with a sharp mustard dressing. If you can't find luganega sausage, another tasty Italian sausage will be fine.

Serves 4

4 baking potatoes, about 7oz (200g) each
olive oil for greasing
3½oz (100g) luganega sausage, casings removed and finely crumbled
5 tbsp light cream
2 garlic cloves, crushed to a purée
2 sprigs fresh rosemary, leaves removed and finely chopped
¾ cup (75g) freshly grated Parmesan cheese
sea salt and freshly ground black pepper

Wash and dry the potatoes thoroughly, then prick them all over with a skewer or a fork. Brush them thoroughly with oil and place them on a lightly oiled sheet of baking parchment on a baking sheet. Place in a preheated oven, 350°F, and bake for an hour or until soft all the way through when you push in a knife. Remove the potatoes from the oven and set aside to cool slightly. Do not turn off the oven.

Cut the top section of each potato off, moving the knife horizontally across the potato, then spoon out the flesh, leaving the skin and enough potato flesh to hold the shape securely. Mash the flesh with the sausage, cream, garlic, rosemary, and half the Parmesan. Season this mixture with salt and pepper and spoon it back into the potatoes. Sprinkle the potatoes with the remaining Parmesan, loosely cover with the removed top sections and return to the oven for a further 10–15 minutes until the sausagemeat is cooked though and the filling is piping hot. Serve at once.

Dried Salt Cod with Roasted Red Bell Pepper and Fennel Salad

Baccalà Mantecato, or *brandade* in French, is not an easy dish to make, but it is very delicious. If you have ever eaten it at any of Venice's many bars, you might have wondered how the Venetian cooks achieve that fantastically smooth, light, fluffy texture. Should you have difficulty in getting the fish going, you can beat it first (after boning and skinning) in a pestle and mortar, or put it in a bowl over a simmering pan of water and mash it with a fork to make it easier to work with. *Baccalà* is dried salted cod, which needs four days of soaking in fresh cold water to reconstitute it, changing the water two or three times each day. (*Stoccafisso*, which is dried salted cod or haddock, is treated in the same way and has a stronger flavor than *baccalà*).

Serves 6

2lb (1 kg) well-soaked dried salted cod or *stoccafisso* (see introduction, above)
about 2 cups (500ml) extra virgin olive oil
4 tbsp finely chopped fresh flat-leaf parsley
4 garlic cloves, 2 crushed to a purée and 2 finely chopped
4 large red bell peppers
4 fennel bulbs, hard outer sections removed
2 tbsp white wine vinegar
sea salt and freshly ground black pepper

Rinse the soaked fish carefully, then put it in a large saucepan and cover with lots of fresh water. Bring to a boil, skimming the surface as necessary, and boil for 15–20 minutes, or a little longer if it still appears tough. Drain the fish, and when it's cool enough to handle, remove all the skin and every single bone.

Transfer the fish flesh to a large bowl and reduce to flakes, then begin to "whip" the fish with a large wooden spoon, gradually adding extra virgin olive oil in a fine stream, as if you are making mayonnaise. (Keep back about 6 tablespoons oil to dress the salad just before serving.) The quantity of oil will depend upon the greasiness of the fish and the quality of the oil, as the lighter the oil is, the less you will need. Stop whipping when the fish has become rather like thick cream, white, light and fluffy. Stir in chopped parsley, crushed garlic, and seasoning to taste, but be very careful not to over-salt—despite all the soaking, the fish will remain fairly salty. Cover and chill until required.

Meanwhile, to make the salad, place the whole peppers in a preheated oven, 350°F, and roast for about 10 minutes until blackened all over.

Remove the peppers from the oven and leave them to steam in a large bowl, sealed with plastic wrap, until completely cool. Skin, seed, and thinly slice the peppers. Return the peppers to the bowl and stir in the chopped garlic and half the remaining oil.

Slice the fennel bulbs very finely and mix with the roasted peppers. Add the remaining oil, the vinegar, and salt and pepper to taste. Cover and chill until required, then serve alongside the *baccalà*.

Tourte aux Blettes
Swiss Chard Tart

Unashamedly French, this is a huge favorite at my cookery school in the Charente. All the local markets sell such glorious-looking Swiss chard (*biete* in Italian, *blettes* in French) that it is impossible not to buy it and rush home to turn it into something delicious … just like this! I like to use the leaves to make a tart or to use as I would use spinach, and the white stalks as a separate vegetable for braising, as I would either celery or fennel bulbs.

Serves 8

For the pastry:

1 cup (140g) all-purpose white flour, plus a little extra for rolling out the pastry

¼ tsp salt

¼ cup (60ml) extra virgin olive oil, plus a little extra for greasing

¼ cup (60ml) water

For the filling:

1 lb (500g) Swiss chard leaves, well washed and dried

3 large eggs

1 cup (100g) freshly grated Parmesan cheese

sea salt and freshly ground black pepper

First, make the pastry. In a large bowl, combine the flour and salt, then add the oil and water, gradually mixing until thoroughly blended. Knead very briefly as the dough will be very soft and moist, like a cookie dough. Shape the dough into a ball, then wrap with very lightly oiled plastic wrap and leave to rest for at least 15 minutes in the refrigerator.

Meanwhile, coarsely chop the Swiss chard with a heavy knife or in the food processor. Place the chard in a large skillet over low heat with salt and pepper to taste and stir constantly until the chard wilts. Whisk the eggs and Parmesan together in a large bowl, then stir in the chard.

Take the pastry out of the refrigerator and let it return to room temperature for about 5 minutes, then roll it out very gently on a lightly floured surface until large enough to line a 11-in (28-cm) pie pan with a removable base. Tip the Swiss chard and egg mixture into the pastry shell.

Place the pie on a baking sheet, put in a preheated oven, 400°F, and bake for 40–45 minutes, until the filling is set and golden brown. Allow to cool, then serve at room temperature.

Cannelloni a Modo Mio
Cannelloni Revisited

This great classic dish is representative of an era of Italian restaurants which, despite all modern influences, seems to remain virtually unchanged. It is hard to imagine, in these days of arugula and balsamic vinegar, and many other oh-so-fashionable ingredients, that something as old-fashioned and comforting as this should still exist. I have revised the recipe to make it less heavy and generally stodgy, while trying to retain the comfort-food aspect, which I am certain is at least part of the story when it comes to the longevity of this dish. There isn't anything spur-of-the-moment about this dish. It has several stages of preparation and takes time, so plan your strategy—the meat filling can be made a day ahead.

Serves 8

1 quantity Basic Pasta Dough
(see page 57)
7oz (200g) fresh mozzarella cheese,
drained and cubed
½ cup (50g) freshly grated Parmesan cheese

For the filling:
1 large onion, finely chopped
1 large carrot, peeled and finely chopped
1 large celery stalk, finely chopped
2 tbsp olive oil
13oz (400g) boneless lean beef or veal
stewing steak, roughly chopped
into small dice
1 glass dry red wine
17fl oz (500ml) passata or crushed canned
tomatoes
1 handful dried porcini mushrooms
sea salt and freshly ground black pepper

For the béchamel sauce:
¾ stick (75g) unsalted butter
4 tbsp all-purpose white flour
2½ cups (600ml) milk
½ cup (50g) freshly grated Parmesan cheese
sea salt
pinch of grated nutmeg

To make the filling, gently fry the onion, carrot, and celery in the oil for about 10 minutes. Add the meat and fry together gently until the meat is well browned. Add the wine and boil quickly for 2 minutes, then stir in the passata or crushed tomatoes and bring to a boil. Reduce the heat to low and simmer, covered, stirring frequently, for about 1½ hours.

While the filling simmers, place the dried mushrooms in a heatproof bowl, pour over enough boiling water to cover and leave to soak for about 30 minutes until reconstituted and tender. Strain the mushrooms through a sieve lined with a double layer of paper towels, or a piece of cheesecloth, and chop coarsely.

Add the mushrooms and the strained liquid to the filling, then season to taste and leave to simmer over very low heat, uncovered, for a further hour, stirring occasionally, until it is dry enough to be rolled up in pieces of pasta, otherwise things can get very messy! (The filling can be left to cool completely at this point and then refrigerated overnight. Reheat it slightly before using.)

Make the pasta dough as instructed on page 57, wrap in plastic wrap and leave to rest for 20 minutes.

Meanwhile, make the béchamel sauce. Melt the butter in a heavy-bottomed saucepan over a medium heat. Add the flour and mix together until a thick yellow paste forms. Pour
in all the milk, whisking briskly to prevent lumps forming. Add the salt and nutmeg to taste, then simmer gently for about 15 minutes, stirring constantly, until the sauce is thick enough to coat the back of a spoon. Remove the pan from the heat, stir in the Parmesan and cover the surface with a little cold water, or a piece of plastic wrap, to prevent a skin from forming; set aside until required.

Roll out the pasta dough until paper thin, as instructed on page 57, then cut into about

20 rectangles about the size of your palm. Cook these in boiling salted water in batches of 3 at a time, just until they rise to the surface of the water, then remove with a slotted spoon or fish slice and lay them carefully on a wet, clean cloth without overlapping. Before long all your kitchen surfaces will be draped with pasta! Keep the cooked pasta moist under wet cloths until required.

Once the meat filling is ready, you can begin to assemble the dish. Cover the base of a large flameproof serving dish with a thin layer of the béchamel sauce. Working with one piece of pasta at a time, spoon about 1½ tablespoons of the filling into the center and add a little mozzarella. Roll up the cannelloni so the filling and cheese are securely enclosed. Place the cannelloni in the dish, seam-side down, then continue rolling cannelloni and adding them to the dish in a single layer. Cover with the remaining béchamel sauce. If necessary, repeat with a second layer, although it is easier to serve this dish if there is only a single layer of cannelloni. Sprinkle the top of the dish with all the remaining Parmesan, then set aside to stand for 10 minutes.

Place the dish on a baking sheet and place in a preheated oven, 400°F, and bake for about 30 minutes until golden brown and bubbling. Remove the dish from the oven and leave to stand for 5 minutes before serving.

Ravioli Giganti con le Cozze
Giant Ravioli with Mussels

I love mussels and fresh pasta, so I created this recipe so I could combine the two elements in a way that balances. The finer the pasta, the better, because the mussels, though strong in taste, need to stand out from the pasta as the main flavor. The slippery quality of the pasta makes the dish incredibly sensuous.

Serves 4

For the pasta:

1½ cups (200g) all-purpose white flour, plus extra for dusting

¾ cup (100g) fine semolina, plus extra for dusting

3 eggs

For the filling:

2⅓lb (1.2kg) fresh mussels

1 red onion, finely chopped

1 glass dry white wine

2 tomatoes, sliced in half

1 bay leaf

1 slice of lemon peel, about 1¼in (3cm) long with all bitter white pith removed

1 handful fresh flat-leaf parsley, chopped

1 cup (250ml) heavy cream

sea salt and freshly ground black pepper

Begin by making the fresh pasta, following the instructions on page 57. Shape the dough into a ball, wrap in plastic wrap and leave to rest for about 20 minutes.

Cut the rested dough in to small sections and roll out, following the instructions on page 57. (Be sure to re-wrap the pasta you are not using while you roll out each section so it doesn't dry out.) Cut the rolled out dough into sixteen 3-in (7-cm) squares and cover with a slightly damp tea towel to stop them drying out—don't overlap the squares.

Next, rinse the mussels well in several changes of water, scrub them and remove their beards. Discard any that are cracked or that do not close when tapped. Place the mussels in a large pot with the red onion, wine, tomatoes, bay leaf, lemon peel, and half the parsley. Cover the pan tightly, and steam over a high heat, shaking occasionally, for about 5 minutes, or until all the mussels have opened. Discard any closed mussels.

Strain the liquid into a wide pan and boil over high heat to reduce to about one-third and set aside. Take all the mussels out of their shells and put them into a bowl; reserve a few of the prettier shells for garnishing the finished dish.

Place a small mound of mussels in the center of each pasta square, lay another square on top [1], trim the edges [2] and seal the ravioli by pinching the 2 pieces together [3]. Bring a large pan of salted water to a rolling boil. Add the ravioli in batches and boil until they are cooked through and floating, then remove and keep warm in a bowl of hot water. Continue until all the ravioli are cooked.

Pour the cream into the reduced cooking liquid and return to the heat. Whisk until thickened, then remove from the heat. Place a little sauce in each of 4 soup plates, then add a ravioli. Cover with more cream, a second ravioli and another layer of cream. Sprinkle with the remaining parsley and garnish with a mussel shell or two. Serve immediately.

Ravioli Aperti con Verdure alla Griglia
Open Ravioli with Broiled Vegetables

When you are slicing the vegetables, pay special attention to the red onion and the fennel, as they'll fall to pieces if you don't leave the root base intact. Don't stint on the olive oil—it will make the vegetables moist and delicious.

Serves 4

1 eggplant, halved and cut into
½-in (1-cm) slices
2 zucchini, cut into ½-in (1-cm) slices
2 red bell peppers, cored, seeded and cut
into ½-in (1-cm) slices
1 large red onion, halved, with the root end
intact, and cut into ½-in (1-cm) slices
1 fennel bulb, halved, with the hard outer
layers removed, cut lengthwise
into ½-in (1-cm) slices
3 garlic cloves, chopped
6 tbsp olive oil
3 tbsp chopped fresh flat-leaf parsley
sea salt and freshly ground black pepper

For the pasta:
1½ cups (200g) all-purpose white flour,
plus extra for dusting
¾ cup (100g) fine semolina, plus extra
for dusting
3 eggs

For the dressing:
½ cup (50g) pine nuts
½ cup freshly grated Parmesan cheese
4 tbsp ricotta cheese

Put the eggplant slices into a colander, sprinkle with salt, and leave to drain in the sink for 30 minutes or so. Put all the other sliced vegetables into a large bowl. Mix the garlic, oil, and parsley together thoroughly, season with salt and pepper and pour this all over the vegetables, then leave to stand for at least an hour, turning occasionally.

Next, make the pasta. Tip the flour and the semolina into a mound on the tabletop and mix them together with your fingertips. Make a well in the center of the mound with your fist. Beat the eggs thoroughly, then pour them into the center of the hollow. Mix the eggs into the flour with your fingers and bring the dough together into a ball, then knead until it is smooth, elastic, and not tacky. Shape the dough into a ball, wrap in plastic wrap and leave to rest for about 20 minutes.

Cut the rested dough in small sections, and roll out, following the instructions on page 57. (Be sure to re-wrap the pasta you are not using while you roll out each section so it doesn't dry out.) Cut the rolled-out dough into sixteen 3-in (7-cm) squares and leave to dry out slightly on a lightly floured surface, without overlapping.

Meanwhile, toast the pine nuts gently in a warm pan over low heat, taking care not to burn them.

Drain the eggplants, rinse, and pat dry. Add to the other vegetables and mix together again to coat completely in dressing. Strain the dressing from the vegetables and put to one side in a small pitcher until required. Top up with a little more olive oil if required; check the seasoning and adjust, if necessary.

Bring a large saucepan of salted water to a rolling boil. Heat a griddle pan until smoking or heat the broiler on high, and warm 4 large plates in a low oven. Griddle or broil all the vegetables in batches until they are cooked and lightly charred, keeping them warm in the low oven. When all the vegetables are tender, cook the pasta quickly in the salted water, in batches, then drain well.

To assemble the dish, drizzle a little dressing on to a warmed plate, place a cooked square of pasta on top, cover with the vegetables and then cover with another square of pasta. Drizzle with the dressing and sprinkle with toasted pine nuts and a little grated Parmesan. Make 2 open ravioli for each plate. Arrange any leftover vegetables around the edges of the plates and place a spoonful of ricotta in the center of each plate just before serving.

Insalata Nizzarda con il Tonno Fresco
Fresh Tuna Niçoise

This is a very smart version of a classic Niçoise, using fresh tuna steaks that are marinated and broiled to a perfect juiciness. The art of this salad lies in the arrangement of all the ingredients on the plate so it looks pretty but not overpowering—go for the largest plates you own!

Serves 4

4 tuna steaks, about 5oz (150g) each, trimmed so they look neat and tidy

10oz (300g) French beans, or other small, young, green beans, topped and tailed

12 very small new potatoes, scrubbed, but not peeled

12 cherry tomatoes, rinsed and hulled

12 quail eggs, hard-cooked, shelled and halved

8 oak leaf lettuce leaves, or other gourmet salad leaves, rinsed and dried

For the marinade:

3 tbsp extra virgin olive oil

1 tsp cracked black pepper

¼ tsp sea salt

freshly squeezed juice of ½ lemon

1 handful fresh herbs, such as parsley, chervil, chives, and basil, finely chopped

For the dressing:

1 shallot, very finely chopped

2 tbsp white wine vinegar

10 tbsp extra virgin olive oil, plus a little extra for grilling

1 tbsp freshly chopped flat-leaf parsley

sea salt and freshly ground black pepper

Mix the marinade ingredients together in a nonmetallic dish large enough to hold the tuna without breaking up. Add the tuna and make sure each steak is coated with the marinade, then set aside until required

Bring 2 saucepans of salted water to a boil. Add the French beans to one pan and the potatoes to the other. Boil the beans for 9 minutes, or until tender, then drain and refresh in cold water. Boil the potatoes for about 12 minutes, or until tender, drain and refresh in cold water, then cut in half.

Meanwhile, make the dressing by mixing the shallot, a pinch of salt, and a little pepper into the vinegar until the salt dissolves. Add the olive oil and parsley and whisk until emulsified and smooth; set aside.

Lightly brush a broiler rack with oil. Place the tuna steaks on top and broil under a preheated broiler for about 3 minutes, depending upon the heat of your broiler and the thickness of the tuna. You should end up with lightly charred tuna steaks with pink, juicy centers.

To serve, arrange 2 lettuce leaves on each of 4 plates. Divide the beans and tuna between the plates, then add 3 halved potatoes, 3 tomatoes, and 6 quail egg halves to each. Whisk the dressing again, if necessary, and drizzle over each plate.

Insalata di Pollo con Fagiolini e Pomodorini

Hot Chicken, Green Bean, and Cherry Tomato Salad

This is an easy dish that somehow always manages to impress. The most important thing is to arrange the salad in a really pretty bowl and to serve it quickly before the salad leaves begin to wilt rather dramatically.

Serves 6

3 small romaine lettuces, broken into leaves

1 oak-leaf or butterhead lettuce, torn into bite-sized pieces

1 head radicchio, torn into bite-sized pieces

12 cherry tomatoes, cut in half

8oz (250g) French beans, or other small, young, green beans, topped and tailed

3 skinless, boneless chicken breasts, cut into finger-sized strips

3 tbsp olive oil

1 garlic clove, crushed

sea salt and freshly ground black pepper

For the dressing:

2 tbsp white wine vinegar

pinch of salt

½ tsp mustard of your choice

10 tbsp extra virgin olive oil

6 grinds of the peppermill

Wash and dry all the salad leaves thoroughly, then arrange them in a wide salad bowl. Scatter the cherry tomatoes through the salad leaves; set aside.

Put all the dressing ingredients in a jelly jar and screw on the lid tightly. Shake the dressing until well mixed and thickened; set aside.

Bring a saucepan of salted water to a boil and cook the beans, uncovered to preserve their color, about 9 minutes or until just tender. Meanwhile, heat the olive oil with the garlic in a large skillet or wok. Add the chicken strips and quickly fry until crisp and the juices run clear when pierced with a knife.

Drain the hot beans, shaking off any excess water, and immediately tip them over the salad leaves. Scatter the hot chicken over the beans. Drizzle with the dressing and serve at once.

Insalata di Rucola con Pere e Parmigiano

Wild Arugula, Pear, and Parmesan Salad

The combination of pears and Parmesan is one of those taste marriages made in heaven. In this salad, the pears play a very important role, so they must be not too ripe, nor too hard. I especially like Kaiser pears, but if they are unavailable Bartlett, Comice, or Bosc are also ideal. This is a good salad to serve after a filling first course. I think it is a good idea to pick over the arugula and remove all those annoyingly long stalks.

Serves 6

6 pears
freshly squeezed juice of 1 lemon
8 tbsp balsamic vinegar
5 handfuls fresh arugula leaves, rinsed, dried and picked over
6oz (175g) fresh Parmesan cheese in a piece, shaved into strips
6 tbsp extra virgin olive oil
sea salt and freshly ground black pepper

Peel, core, and thinly slice the pears. Place them in a bowl and toss with the lemon juice to coat them completely to prevent them turning brown; set aside.

Reduce the balsamic vinegar by boiling it quickly in a skillet until it is reduced by about two-thirds to give you about 2 tablespoons. This will make the most thin and sour balsamic taste sweet and deep.

Put the arugula leaves in the salad bowl with the Parmesan and toss together gently, using your hands. Beat the balsamic vinegar with the olive oil and salt and pepper to taste, using a fork or a small whisk, until emulsified. Drain the pears and pour the liquid into the dressing, then whisk again.

Add the pears to the arugula leaves and the Parmesan and mix together gently with your hands. Drizzle over the dressing, and mix again to make sure the dressing has coated the pears as well as the arugula. Serve at once before the salad wilts.

Insalata di Radicchio, Arance e Noci

Radicchio, Orange, and Walnut Salad

A salad with lots of flavors and textures all going on at once, so ideally this is best served on its own or alongside a selection of amazing blue cheeses with some really good bread. Naturally, the overall effect of the salad is dependent upon the individual ingredients being really good to begin with.

Serves 6

3 heads radicchio, rinsed, dried, trimmed, and finely shredded

about 20 fresh walnuts, shelled and halved

5 large oranges

2 tbsp reduced balsamic vinegar (see page 80)

large pinch sea salt

freshly ground black pepper

6 tbsp extra virgin olive oil

Put the radicchio and walnuts in a salad bowl and toss together with your hands. To prepare the oranges, slice off the bases and pare away the peel and all the white pith. Working over a bowl, slice between each membrane to remove the orange segments. Allow each segment to fall into the salad but catch the juice to add to the dressing.

Quickly whisk together the balsamic vinegar, salt, pepper, and olive oil with any saved orange juice. Drizzle this over the salad, toss together just enough to coat the salad lightly and serve at once.

Funghi al Verde

Parsley Mushrooms

This is a very simple and delicious way of preparing mushrooms, which you can use for filling an omelet, or as an accompaniment for chicken or any meat.

Serves 6

½ stick (50g) unsalted butter

3–4 tbsp olive oil

1 large handful fresh flat-leaf parsley, chopped

1 garlic clove, chopped

1lb (500g) fresh porcini (cèpes) mushrooms, cleaned, trimmed, and thinly sliced

sea salt and freshly ground black pepper

Melt the butter and oil together, then add the parsley and garlic and fry slowly for about 5 minutes, stirring. Add all the mushrooms, season with a little salt and pepper, cover the pan tightly and leave to simmer very slowly for about 30 minutes. Serve at once.

4 relaxing over dinner

This is the chapter that contains some of my most long-winded recipes, those which are truly indulgent in terms of both the cooking and the eating. Unashamedly, I can tell you that some dishes, such as the *Timballo di Pasta* for instance, might take you an entire day to assemble, if not longer! These are dishes which might present a bit of a challenge, but which are not difficult to prepare, just need love and understanding and some patience. I'd like to think that everybody will cook these dishes at least once, and that some of them might even become firm favorites. I think it's always a good idea to involve a friend or a family member to help you when undertaking a big recipe. It makes the whole experience much more fun and gives you someone else to blame should things go slightly awry!

Tonno alla Calabrese

Tuna in the Calabrian style

This is an unusual way of serving fresh tuna, but typical of all Calabrian cuisine the end result is spicy hot with chili. It is absolutely delicious with a mound of mashed potatoes and a bottle of robust red wine. I sometimes add other ingredients to the basic sauce, such as capers, olives, or a generous pinch or two of dried oregano.

Serves 4

4 tuna steaks, about 7oz (200g) each, rinsed and patted dry
2 tbsp all-purpose white flour
4 tbsp olive oil
4 tbsp dry white wine
2oz (50g) pancetta, finely chopped
1–2 dried red chili peppers, chopped
1 onion chopped with 1 large garlic clove
2 tbsp chopped fresh flat-leaf parsley
4 anchovy fillets preserved in oil or salt, rinsed
10oz (300g) canned tomatoes, seeded and chopped
sea salt and freshly ground black pepper

Season the tuna steaks thoroughly on both sides with salt and pepper, then lightly coat on both sides with the flour, shaking off any excess.

Heat the oil in a wide skillet over medium heat. Add the tuna steaks and fry for 3 minutes on each side. Splash in the wine and allow the alcohol to boil off for 1 minute. Transfer the fish to paper towels to drain and set aside.

Put the pancetta, chili, onion and garlic, and half the parsley in the oil and fry gently for about 5 minutes, stirring occasionally. Add the anchovy fillets and mash them into the hot oil with a fork. After a minute or so, add the tomatoes and stir together thoroughly. Season and simmer, half covered with a lid, for about 15 minutes, until the sauce reduces slightly.

Slide the tuna into the pan and heat through for about 8 minutes, turning them over gently once. Transfer the tuna onto a warmed dish, cover with the sauce, and sprinkle with the remaining parsley just before serving.

Lasagna di Magro al Pesce con il Granchio

Fish and Crab Lasagne

This is a wonderfully luxurious lasagne, filling and rich. It only needs a crisp salad as an accompaniment. You can, of course, substitute the crab for lobster meat for an even more deluxe dish.

Serves 6

1 quantity Basic Pasta Dough (see page 57)
1 tsp olive oil

For the filling:
1 onion, sliced
5 tbsp olive oil
2 zucchini, diced
2 carrots, peeled and diced
1 cup (100g) shelled peas, thawed if frozen
3½oz (100g) button mushrooms, wiped and sliced
1 medium–large tomato, skinned and chopped
12oz (350g) poached white fish, such as cod, halibut, or haddock, carefully skinned, boned, and flaked
8oz (250g) white fresh or canned crab meat
½ cup (50g) freshly grated Parmesan cheese
5oz (150g) fresh mozzarella cheese, drained and sliced

For the béchamel sauce:
¾ stick (70g) unsalted butter
⅝ cup (70g) all-purpose white flour
4 cups (1 liter) milk
sea salt
pinch of freshly grated nutmeg

First make the pasta as described on page 57. Shape into a ball, wrap in plastic wrap and leave to rest for at least 20 minutes.

Meanwhile, make the béchamel sauce as described on page 72, but omit adding any Parmesan cheese. Cover with a thin layer of cold water, or a piece of plastic wrap directly on the surface, to prevent a skin forming and set aside until required.

Cut the rested dough into sections and roll out until paper thin, following the instructions on page 57. (Be sure to re-wrap the pasta you are not using while you roll out each section so it doesn't dry out.) Cut the dough into about 20 rectangles about the size of your palm and leave to dry slightly on a lightly floured surface, without overlapping. Cook these in boiling salted water in batches of 3 at a time just until they rise to the surface of the water, then remove with a slotted spoon or fish slice and lay them carefully on a wet, clean cloth, without overlapping. Cover the pasta with a damp cloth to prevent it drying out until required.

To make the filling, fry the onion in the oil until soft. Add the zucchini, carrots, and peas and continue frying, uncovered and stirring together, until the vegetables are tender. Keep a close eye on the pan and add a little water as required. Season to taste.

To assemble the dish, spread a layer of béchamel into a greased shallow ovenproof serving dish. Cover the base of the dish with a layer of pasta sheets, then add the first layer of cooked vegetables and a handful of raw mushrooms followed by a handful of raw chopped tomato. Scatter over a layer of flaked fish and crabmeat, sprinkle lightly with Parmesan and then cover with another layer of béchamel sauce. Repeat these layers until all ingredients are used, then add a final layer of mozzarella and a final sprinkling of Parmesan.

Place the dish in a preheated oven, 400°F, and bake for 35–45 minutes until golden brown on top and heated through. Leave to rest for 10 minutes before serving.

Trota in Crosta di Mandorle

Trout with an Almond Crust

Sometimes I ring the changes with this dish and use hazelnuts instead of almonds. I have a lot of practice in coming up with ideas for cooking trout, as I spent every summer of my childhood fishing them in the lochs of Connemara and Mayo.

Serves 4

1 large shallot, finely chopped
3½ tbsp all-purpose white flour
1 cup (75g) ground almonds
2½oz (65g) fresh rosemary leaves, rinsed, dried, and finely chopped
1 stick (100g) unsalted butter, softened
4 fresh trout, about 8oz (250g) each, cleaned and gutted
1½ cups (150g) slivered almonds
olive oil for greasing
4 tbsp dry white wine
½ cup (100ml) sour cream
sea salt and freshly ground black pepper

Mix the shallot with the flour, ground almonds, and half the rosemary leaves. Work this into the butter and add seasoning to taste. Divide the mixture in half and roll one half into 4 small balls, then tuck one ball into each of the trout. Spread the rest of the butter mixture over the fish. Press the fish on both sides into the slivered almonds, making sure the almonds stick securely to the fish.

Line an ovenproof dish with lightly greased baking parchment and lay the fish on top of the paper in a single layer. Place in a preheated oven, 425°F, and bake for 5 minutes. Remove the dish from the oven, turn the fish over very carefully and bake for a further 5 minutes.

Gently transfer the fish to a warmed serving platter and pour the juices from the baking dish into a small pan. Add the remaining rosemary leaves and the wine and bring to a boil, swirling the pan. Boil the wine for one minute to evaporate the alcohol, then stir in the sour cream and return to a low bubble, swirling the pan around rather than stirring. Pour this sauce around the fish and serve.

Riso e Cozze

Rice and Mussels

A really delicious dish I discovered at a simple lunch time *tavola calda* (an old-fashioned, genuine Italian fast-food joint) attached to a bakery in the town of Monopoli in Puglia. I have always thought that the nutty taste of rice and the sweet/salty flavor of fresh mussels makes a fantastic combination.

Serves 6

1lb (500g) risotto rice

1 large onion, coarsely chopped

5 tbsp extra virgin olive oil

2lb (1kg) fresh mussels, well scrubbed with beards removed and rinsed in several changes of water

1 glass dry white wine

1 handful chopped fresh flat-leaf parsley

about 10 cherry tomatoes, washed and halved

fish stock (optional)

sea salt and freshly ground black pepper

Bring a large saucepan of salted water to a boil. Add the rice and boil for about 8 minutes, then drain and rinse through briefly with hot water to remove only some of the starch.

Meanwhile, fry the onion in half the oil in a large pan for about 6 minutes until the onion is semisoft. Discard any mussels with cracked shells or open ones that don't close when tapped, then add the rest to the pan with the wine, parsley, and salt and pepper to taste. Tightly cover the pan and steam over high heat for 8 minutes, shaking the pan occasionally, or until all the mussels have opened. Discard any unopened mussels, then strain carefully through a sieve lined with cheesecloth or a double layer of paper towels and reserve the liquid. Discard any sediment that is left after straining.

Lightly grease an ovenproof dish large enough to hold all the mussels and the rice together. Shell most of the mussels and stir these into the semicooked rice. Stir in all the strained liquid, the tomatoes, and half the remaining oil. Reserve a few mussels in their shells to garnish the top of the dish.

Spoon the rice mixture into the dish and arrange the mussels in their shells around the top, facing downward so they are embedded in the rice. Drizzle with the remaining oil and cover loosely with foil. Place in a preheated oven, 375°F, and bake for about 20 minutes, or until the rice is tender. Check halfway through the cooking time, and if the rice appears too dry, add a little fish stock. Serve at once.

Fritto Misto
Fried Fish and Vegetables

For this recipe, you need an open, airy space in which to fry all the various ingredients. The following quantities are enough to feed about eight people, but vary the ingredients and quantities according to availability and your own taste.

Serves 8

2½lb (1.2kg) small fish, such as whitebait (smelt), mixed with large raw unpeeled shrimp

2lb (1kg) mixed fresh vegetables, such as artichokes, very firm tomatoes, bell peppers, zucchini, fennel, rinsed, trimmed and cut into equal-sized pieces about 2½ x1¾ inches (6 x 4cm)

6 sprigs fresh basil, rinsed and dried

6 sprigs fresh sage, rinsed and dried

5oz (150g) mozzarella cheese, drained and cut into chunks

3½–5¼ pints (2–3 liters) sunflower oil

sea salt

lemon wedges to serve

For the batter:

5 eggs, beaten

8 tbsp all-purpose white flour

pinch of salt

3 cups (750ml) milk

First make the batter. Beat the eggs with a balloon whisk until well blended and smooth. Gradually add the flour and the salt, beating constantly, then gradually beat in the milk, until a lump-free batter forms. (You might discover as you go along that annoyingly you don't have enough, in which case you will have to allow enough time to repeat this procedure to make more.)

Make sure all the ingredients for frying are as dry as possible. Divide the batter between 3 large bowls. Put the fish in one, the vegetables in another, and the cheese and herbs in the third. Submerge them all in the batter and let them stand for about 30 minutes.

Divide the oil between 2 or 3 deep-fat fryers or deep skillets. Lay out plenty of paper towels to absorb the excess oil on a large serving platter over a big saucepan of boiling water—this keeps all the ingredients warm without allowing the food to go soggy.

Heat the oil until a small piece of bread dropped into the oil sizzles instantly. Fry the fish in one pan of fat, and the other ingredients in a second pan. Fry them all quickly, in batches, turning them over after about 2 minutes and fishing them out with a slotted spoon as soon as they are golden and crisp. Work quickly and keep the oil at maximum heat so everything cooks as fast as possible. Drain on the paper towels and sprinkle with sea salt. Serve immediately on a warm platter with the lemon wedges.

Valentina's Pasta Pie

Valentina's Timballo di Pasta

The whole idea of this spectacularly rich and sumptuous dish is that the slightly sweet pastry must contrast with the salty, savory filling. The sharper the contrast, the better the finished effect. The pastry case must be chunky thick but also very, very crumbly and light. I think probably the most difficult part of the whole operation is lining the pan with the paper, then gingerly extracting the pie without cracking or breaking it. This is a dish inspired by the *pasticcio di maccheroni* of my mother's Tuscan childhood, when three days were set aside for the careful preparation of this luxurious treat for that very special day when the bishop came to lunch! Allow at least four hours to prepare this dish, and a further 45 minutes baking time.

Serves 8–10 (makes a 10-in (25-cm) round pie)

For the pastry:

1¾lb + 2 tbsp (900g), about 7 cups, all-purpose white flour, sifted twice, plus extra for dusting

4 sticks (500g) unsalted butter, diced, plus extra for generously greasing the tin

4 tbsp superfine sugar

7 egg yolks

¼ tsp salt

For the mushrooms:

10oz (300g) mushrooms, such as cremini, porcini (cèpes), field or oyster

¾ cup (200ml) water

2 shallots, very finely sliced

¼ stick (25g) unsalted butter

1 heaping tbsp chopped fresh flat-leaf parsley

For the sauce :

1 tbsp unsalted butter

3 heaping tbsp all-purpose white flour, sifted

1¼ cups (300ml) dry white wine

1¾ cups (400ml) light cream

¾ cup (200ml) milk

¼ tsp salt

¼ tsp ground white pepper

½ tsp ground mace

1 cup (100g) freshly grated Parmesan cheese

(Continued...)

To make the pastry, tip the flour onto the work surface and make a hollow in the center with your fist. Put the butter into the hollow. Add the sugar, egg yolks, and salt and knead together until you have achieved the texture of soft marzipan (almond paste): do not over-knead. Gently roll the pastry into a ball, put it in a bowl and leave it to rest somewhere not too warm and not too cool until you have got all the filling ingredients nearly ready: do not put it in the refrigerator. On a cool window sill is a good place.

To prepare the mushrooms, peel them all carefully and put the skin in a small saucepan. Next, trim the mushrooms and add the trimmings to the pan. Slice the mushrooms evenly and set aside. Add the water to the pan, half cover, and simmer for 20 minutes. Strain through cheesecloth and keep warm until required—you should end up with about 6 tablespoons of liquid. Slowly fry the shallots in the butter until they are softened. Add the mushrooms and stir to cover in butter and shallots. Season with salt and simmer, covered, for about 10 minutes or until the mushrooms are soft and have absorbed all the liquid. Sprinkle with parsley, check the seasoning, stir, and set aside.

Now make the sauce. Melt the butter in a large pan until foaming. Stir in the flour with a balloon whisk until you have a smooth paste. Pour in the wine and whisk together thoroughly to make a completely smooth sauce base, then boil for about 2 minutes, whisking constantly. Add the cream and whisk thoroughly to blend it into the sauce, then stir in the milk and the reserved mushroom liquid. Reduce the heat and add the salt, pepper, and mace. Simmer for 10–15 minutes, stirring. Stir in the Parmesan, then set aside until required with a thin layer of cold water on top to prevent a skin forming.

Next, prepare the fillings. Broil the chicken breasts and slice them into thin strips. Bring 2 pans of salted water to a boil. Meanwhile, warm the melted butter in a pan over medium heat, then add the chicken pieces and stir to coat well. (This is simply to make sure they are not dry.) Season to taste, then stir the chicken into the mushrooms, and set aside. Add the peas and the asparagus spears to separate pans of boiling water and boil until they are tender, then drain well and set aside separately.

Arrange the chicken and mushroom mixture, peas, asparagus, mozzarella, and penne in a neat row on a work surface, with plenty of room to work.

For the filling:

¼ stick (25g) unsalted butter, melted
3 skinless, boneless chicken breasts
1½ cups (200g) petit pois or shelled fresh peas
8oz (250g) asparagus spears, trimmed
10oz (300g) fresh mozzarella cheese, drained and diced
1½lb (750g) fresh penne
½ cup (50g) freshly grated Parmesan cheese
3 tbsp light cream

1 egg, beaten, to glaze
salad or hot green vegetables to serve

Line the base and side of a 10-in (25-cm) springform cake pan with flat, smooth baking parchment that has been buttered on both sides and set aside. Now line the pan with the pastry. Be aware that every time you move the pastry it will split, crumble, and break! Try to handle it as little as you can and work quickly. Do not attempt to roll it out less than ¾-in (2-cm) thick. Divide the pastry into 3 equal-sized pieces. Lightly flour your surface and use a rolling pin to roll out one-third into a circle that will generously line the base, so the pastry comes some of the way up the sides. Divide the second piece of pastry into 6 lumps and position these lumps at equal distances around the edge. Press them out flat, using all 4 fingers, with your thumb on the outside of the pan, so they eventually all spread far enough to overlap [1]; trim off any excess and set aside. The pan should now be thickly covered on the base and sides. Roll out the remaining dough into a thick circle that will form the lid; set aside. Roll all the leftover scraps of pastry into a ball (you should have a lump about the size of a large apple), wrap in plastic wrap and leave it to rest again until needed. Set aside the pastry-lined pan in a cool place.

Bring another large pan of salted water to a boil. Toss in the pasta and boil it for about a minute less than normal so it is very *al dente*. Drain it really very thoroughly and return it to the pot. Pour over almost all the sauce and mix it together thoroughly.

Pour half the pasta into the pastry-lined pan. Cover with the mushrooms and chicken mixture, asparagus, peas, and the mozzarella [2]. Sprinkle with about half the Parmesan and drizzle over the cream. Cover with the remaining pasta [3]. Sprinkle with the

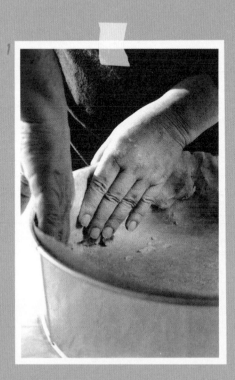

remaining sauce and the remaining Parmesan. Bang the pan down gently to settle the contents. Cover the top with the pastry lid [4, 5, 6] and lightly pinch the edges together all the way around. There will be many holes! Solve this by lightly rolling out the ball of leftover pastry and coil it all the way around the edge over the join. Press it down firmly with a fork all the way around to seal the pie. Roll out any remaining pastry and cut it into whatever shapes you like, then arrange these on top as decoration. Brush the top thoroughly with beaten egg to glaze.

Preheat the oven to 350°F. Carefully slide the *timballo* onto a baking sheet (remember the pan has a loose base so be really careful not to push upward and split the pastry). Place on the center shelf and bake for 35 minutes. Increase the heat to 425°F and bake for a further 15 minutes, or until golden brown. Keep an eye on the *timballo* at all times and do not let it burn!

Slide the *timballo* out of the oven and cool for about 5 minutes before attempting to remove from the pan. If you don't have a springform pan, which will simply require unclipping and sliding off the metal base, place the baking pan on top of a large, heavy can or jar. The sides should slide down, or it should be quite simple to gently ease them down. Slide the pie off the base onto a flat serving dish, perhaps with the help of a fish slice or large palette knife. Just take your time! Very carefully remove the paper wherever visible, but don't worry about leaving the paper underneath the pie. Serve warm, sliced into generous wedges with salad or green vegetables.

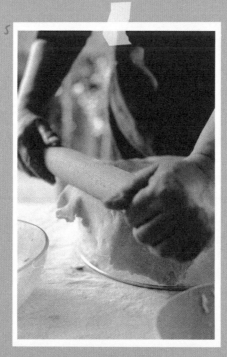
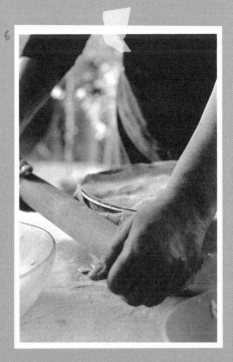

Pollo Arrosto con Olive Nere

Roasted Chicken with Black Olives

If you like the taste of black olives you'll love this way of roasting a chicken, as the bird becomes completely permeated with the flavor of the olives, from the inside out! Be sure to use olives preserved in olive oil with plenty of fragrant herbs.

Serves 6

7oz (200g) black olives marinated in herbs, pitted

2 thick slices pancetta, coarsely ground

1 roasting chicken, about 4lb (2kg), wiped

1 sprig fresh rosemary, leaves removed and finely chopped

1 sprig fresh tarragon, leaves removed and finely chopped

1 large sprig fresh thyme, leaves removed and finely chopped

2 garlic cloves, finely chopped

6 tbsp extra virgin olive oil, plus a little extra for the pan

2 glasses dry white wine

sea salt and freshly ground black pepper

Combine the olives and pancetta and use to stuff the cavity of the chicken. Sew the chicken closed securely. Combine the herbs with the garlic and enough olive oil to create a thick paste, then season to taste. Very carefully slide your hand under the chicken's breast skin on both sides to loosen the skin, then slip the herb-and-garlic paste under the skin and pat into an even layer.

Oil a roasting pan and lay the chicken breast side down in the pan. Drizzle over the remaining oil and season the chicken all over with salt and pepper, then pour in half the wine. Place the pan in a preheated oven, 350°F, and roast for 35 minutes. Turn the chicken over, pour over the rest of the wine and continue to roast for a further 30 minutes (more or less, depending upon the size of the chicken), until the chicken is cooked through and the juices run clear when you pierce the thickest part of the leg with a knife or skewer.

Transfer the chicken to a warmed serving platter, rest for a few minutes, and then carve to serve, reserving all the remaining cooking juices in a small bowl or sauceboat as a simple sauce to go with the chicken.

Rabbit Roasted with Mustard and Pancetta

Rabbit is a delicious meat, lean and sweet tasting. I like to cook it in various different ways—most ways of casseroling chicken, for example, can easily be adapted for the preparation of tasty rabbit dishes. Here is one possibility, and for those of you who really can't bear the idea of cooking rabbit, try chicken joints instead! The end result should be like a dry roast, not a wet casserole with sauce around it, but the meat should remain moist and succulent.

Serves 4

1 rabbit, about 2½lb (1.25kg), skinned, jointed, rinsed and dried
1 bay leaf
1 onion, quartered
3 sprigs fresh thyme
4 garlic cloves, sliced
3–4 tbsp Dijon mustard
7oz (200g) sliced pancetta or fatty bacon
2 sprigs fresh rosemary
3 tbsp extra virgin olive oil
2 tbsp fresh white breadcrumbs
a little vegetable or chicken stock or water (optional)
1–2 tbsp white wine vinegar
1 glass dry white wine
sea salt and freshly ground black pepper

Place the rabbit pieces in a deep bowl with the bay leaf, onion, 2 of the thyme sprigs and one of the garlic cloves. Turn the rabbit joints over with your hands to make sure the marinade ingredients coat them all. Cover and leave to stand for about 1 hour.

Remove the rabbit joints and, using a pastry brush, cover each one generously in a layer of mustard. Wrap each mustard-coated joint in a slice of pancetta.

Arrange the wrapped joints in an ovenproof dish with the remaining garlic cloves, the rosemary sprigs, and the remaining thyme sprig distributed between them. Sprinkle with the olive oil, season with salt and pepper, and scatter the breadcrumbs on top. Loosely cover the top with a sheet of crumpled, wet baking parchment.

Place the dish in a preheated oven, 350°F, and roast for about 35 minutes, turning the joints over once during cooking, until the rabbit is cooked through and the juices run clear when pierced with the tip of a knife. If the rabbit appears to be drying out, dampen it slightly by basting with a little warm water or stock.

Remove the rabbit pieces from the dish and keep them warm. Strain the cooking juices into a separate pan. Add the vinegar and the wine and bring to a boil and boil fast for about 2 minutes. Season to taste. Drizzle the sauce over the rabbit and serve at once.

Roasted Veal with Vin Santo

This way of roasting veal is truly delicious, and the same method can also be adopted for pork. I love veal and cannot understand why it isn't eaten a great deal more outside of Italy and France.

Serves 8

1 veal joint, about 3½lb (1.75kg), wiped

1 handful of fresh sage leaves, finely chopped

3 garlic cloves, peeled and cut into sticks

1 bottle vin santo

sea salt and freshly ground black pepper

Pierce the veal joint all over with a sharp knife or skewer. Mix 3 pinches of salt and plenty of pepper together and insert into the holes in the meat, then push the sage leaves and garlic into the holes.

Place the meat in a roasting pan and pour over half the wine. Place in a preheated oven, 400°F, and roast for 45–60 minutes, turning the meat frequently and pouring over more wine as it roasts. When the meat is cooked it should still be pink in the middle and surrounded by a sticky, dark sauce created by the meat juices mingling with the sweet wine. If necessary, put the roasting pan over medium heat on the hob and stir to reduce the juices slightly.

Rest the joint for a few minutes before carving, then slice the meat onto a warmed platter, pour half the juices over the meat, and serve the rest in a sauceboat.

Costata di Vitello o di Maiale con Zucca e Funghi al Formaggio

Veal or Pork Chops with Pumpkin, Mushrooms, and Cheese

The tricky bit here is to make the cut in the meat deep enough so that the filling doesn't fall out during the cooking process. You might be better off asking your butcher to do this for you. Once you have explained how you are going to cook the meat he'll know exactly what to do.

Serves 4

3½ oz (100g) spinach leaves, rinsed

7oz (200g) pumpkin or butternut squash, peeled and seeded

4 bone-in veal or pork rib chops, weighing about 8oz (250g) each

1oz (25g) dried porcini mushrooms, soaked in warm water for about 30 minutes

½ stick (60g) unsalted butter

2 tbsp olive oil

1 large shallot, chopped

1 cup (100g) Gruyère or Emmenthal cheese, cubed

3½ tbsp dry white wine

1 small onion, chopped

sea salt and freshly ground black pepper

Put the spinach leaves in a saucepan over medium-high heat with just the water clinging to their leaves and a pinch of salt. Heat, stirring occasionally, until they wilt and become very tender. Drain the spinach leaves, squeeze dry when cool enough to handle, chop them and set aside.

Meanwhile, cut half the pumpkin into cubes and thinly slice the remaining half; set aside

Slit the chops horizontally, without cutting all the way through, to create a deep pocket in each, but making sure the chops retain their shape; set aside.

Strain the mushrooms through fine cheesecloth or a double layer of paper towels, and reserve the liquid. Chop the mushrooms and put them into a skillet with half the butter, the oil, and the shallot. Fry together gently for 5 minutes, then add the cubed pumpkin and continue to stir over medium heat until it is soft. Stir in the spinach and heat through.

Take the pan off the heat and allow the mixture to cool slightly, then stir in the cheese and season to taste.

Divide the pumpkin and spinach mixture into 4 equal portions and use to stuff the chops, then close the openings and secure with wooden toothpicks.

Melt the remaining butter in a large skillet and fry the stuffed chops until brown and sealed on both sides. Add the wine and boil off the alcohol for 1 minute, then add the onion, the sliced pumpkin, and seasoning to taste. Cover the pan and leave to simmer for about 10 minutes, until the chops are cooked and the pumpkin is tender.

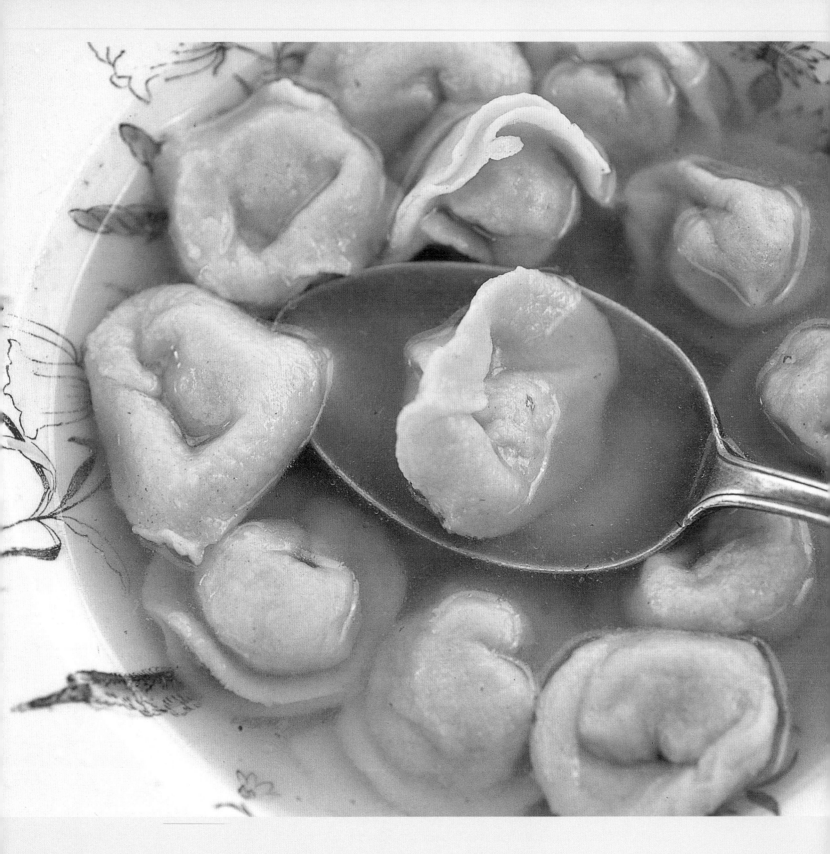

Tortellini in Broth

This dish is the pride of the city of Bologna. It looks simple, but requires quite a lot of work and various different elements to bring it all to the table. In this recipe for pasta dough, salt is used to make it slightly stiffer than usual, so that the tortellini hold their shape while cooking. Once made, you can open-freeze the tortellini on trays, then put them in a bag and leave in the freezer for up to one month and cook from frozen, although they won't be quite as good as the fresh version.

Serves about 10

sea salt and freshly ground black pepper
freshly grated Parmesan cheese to serve

For the broth:

1 large boiling fowl or capon washed and ready to cook
3 carrots, peeled, topped and tailed
3 onions, halved
2 celery stalks, trimmed
2 tomatoes, halved
2 cabbage leaves, rinsed
1 handful fresh flat-leaf parsley sprigs
7 pints (4 liters) cold water

For the filling:

½ stick (50g) unsalted butter
4oz (115g) pork loin, diced
2oz (50g) skinless, boneless turkey breast, diced
4oz (115g) mortedella, in one piece, casing removed
4oz (115g) prosciutto crudo, ideally Parma ham, in one piece
2 eggs, beaten
1½ cups (175g) freshly grated Parmesan
large pinch of freshly grated nutmeg

For the pasta:

2⅔ cups (350g) all-purpose white flour
2½ cups (350g) fine semolina
small pinch of fine sea salt
7 eggs, beaten

To make the broth, place the bird in a large pot with the vegetables and a little salt. Slowly bring to a boil, skimming the surface as necessary, then cover and leave to simmer gently for about 2 hours. Remove the pot from the heat and leave the liquid and flavoring ingredients to cool in the pot.

Once the broth is cool, lift out the bird and set aside. Strain the stock through fine cheesecloth or a double layer of paper towels. Leave the stock to stand until cooled, remove any fat that might form on the top and strain again: you will need about 6 pints (3.6 liters). Meanwhile, to make the filling for the pasta, melt the butter in a large pan over medium-high heat. Add the pork and turkey and fry for about 10 minutes, stirring frequently, until cooked through. Transfer to a hand grinder, add the mortadella and ham and grind 3 times until well mixed and finely ground. (Alternatively, whiz all the ingredients in a food processor, but this is not ideal because the texture will be too smooth.) Stir in the eggs, Parmesan, nutmeg, and salt and pepper to taste. Mix together very thoroughly, then set aside until required. (This is traditionally used to fill tortellini, but can also be used with ravioli, agnolotti, cannelloni, or any shape of your choice.)

To make the pasta for the tortellini, tip the flour, semolina, and salt into a mound on the work surface and mix them together with your fingertips. Make a well in the center of the mound with your fist. Pour the eggs into the center of the hollow. Mix the eggs into the flour with your fingers and bring the dough together into a ball, then knead until it is smooth, elastic, and not tacky. Remember you are not making pastry, so don't be too delicate. Shape the dough into a ball, wrap in plastic wrap and leave to rest for about 20 minutes.

Roll out the pasta dough as described on page 57, using a rolling pin or a pasta machine. Lay the sheet of pasta carefully on to a very lightly floured surface and cover the pasta you are not working with a clean towel. You must cut and fill the pasta immediately to prevent it drying out too much: it is impossible to fill and seal dry pasta. To shape the pasta, use a 1½-in (4-cm) round cookie cutter to cut out about as many circles as you can.

(Continued...)

Put ¼ teaspoon filling in the center of a dough circle [1]. Fold the dough in half and hold between your middle and index fingers. Wrap the two extremities around the tip of your index finger, then push the filled pasta pocket off your finger and turn it half inside out so it looks like a little belly button [2]. Press the ends together and proceed to the next one, continuing until all the filling is used [3].

To assemble, bring the broth to a boil in a large saucepan over high heat. Add the tortellini, then reduce the heat and simmer until they are tender. Remove the pan from the heat and ladle the soup out into individual bowls or transfer to a soup tureen. It is normal practice in Italy to ask people whether they would prefer their tortellini with more or less brodo and to serve them accordingly. Offer freshly grated Parmesan separately at the table.

Variation

The tortellini can also be shaped as squares, if you like. Work with one strip of pasta at a time, keeping the other strips covered. Cut into equal-sized squares, the smaller the better, although too small will mean you can't make the tortellini at all! Cut out just a couple of squares of different sizes to begin with, to see what size works best for you. I find 1¾in (4cm) works best for me. Drop ¼ teaspoon of the filling in the center of a square, then fold in half to make a triangle and seal the edges by pressing together with your finger tips. If the pasta is beginning to dry out, dab the edges with a little bit of cold water to moisten and help seal.

Cosciotto d'Agnello all'Aglio

Slow Roasted Leg of Lamb with Garlic

I like to make this dish in my old brick, a very 1970s terracotta cooking item that was originally meant to cook chicken, and which is permeated with the flavors of a thousand meals! If you can't find an oven-proof dish large enough to take the leg of lamb whole, you could try dividing it in half or using a different part of the lamb such as the knuckle or shoulder.

Serves 8

2 large onions, thickly sliced
2 celery stalks, coarsely chopped
2 carrots, peeled and coarsely chopped
50 garlic cloves, peeled but left whole
4 tbsp olive oil
2 bay leaves
1 large sprig fresh rosemary, leaves removed
6 leaves fresh sage
1 leg of lamb, about 6lb (3kg)
1 bottle dry white wine
2 cups (500ml) meat or vegetable stock, warm
sea salt and freshly ground black pepper

Put the onions, celery, carrots, and all the garlic with the olive oil in an ovenproof casserole dish large enough to hold the leg of lamb and all the ingredients comfortably. Fry the vegetables, stirring frequently, until just softened. Stir in the bay leaves, rosemary and sage, and season with salt and pepper.

Add the leg of lamb to the casserole and turn it over several times to brown it thoroughly on all sides. If necessary, take out all of the vegetables to make room for the lamb and then return them to the casserole. Pour half the wine over the lamb and boil fast to evaporate the alcohol. Season the lamb.

Cover the casserole and place it in a preheated oven, 350°F, and cook for about 3 hours or until the lamb is almost falling off the bone. During the cooking time, turn the lamb over several times and baste with the rest of the wine and stock.

When the lamb is tender, transfer it to a warmed platter to carve. Put the remaining contents of the casserole in a food processor or blender and whiz until smooth. Serve the resulting sauce with the lamb.

Filetto di Maiale in Crosta di Patate e Sedano Rapa

Pork Tenderloin in a Potato and Celeriac Crust

Pork tenderloin is usually very tender, but not especially full of flavor. By wrapping it up in a soft potato and celeriac crust, not only are the flavors of the meat intensified, but the meat also takes on the flavors of other ingredients as it cooks, without losing any of the tenderness. This is really delicious and perfect with a creamy potato dish and some braised cabbage.

Serves 4

1¾lb (875g) pork tenderloin, trimmed and any skin removed
¼ stick (25g) unsalted butter
2 tbsp extra virgin olive oil
1 heaping tbsp mustard of your choice
2 large potatoes, peeled
7oz (200g) celeriac, peeled
3 tbsp all-purpose white flour
pinch of dried thyme
sea salt and freshly ground black pepper

Tie the pork tenderloin into a neat joint with kitchen string.

Melt the butter with the olive oil in a large skillet. Add the pork and brown on all sides to seal. Remove the meat from the pan, leave to cool completely and then cut off the string. Spread the surface with the mustard.

Meanwhile, using a mandolin or the fine julienne attachment of a food processor, cut the potatoes and celeriac into fine julienne slices. Put the slices in a bowl, add the flour and season to taste with salt and pepper. Use your hand to mix together. Tip the potato and celeriac mixture on to a sheet of baking parchment large enough to wrap the meat in and spread the mixture out to cover the surface of the paper. Sprinkle on the thyme.

Wrap the paper and the julienne layer around the meat securely, tying the ends with string, then transfer carefully to a roasting pan. Place the roasting pan in a preheated oven, 400°F, and roast for 40 minutes. Remove from the oven and leave to stand for 10 minutes, then unwrap and slice carefully to serve.

Polenta al Forno con Ragù e i Porcini

Baked Polenta with Pork Ragù and Porcini Mushrooms

For this classic winter warmer you will need to cook the polenta the old-fashioned way, with lots of time and plenty of stirring energy! I try to avoid quick-cook polenta as much as I can, as it doesn't even come close to having the flavor and texture of the real thing. This dish comes from the northernmost regions of Italy, yet the wine you should pair it with needs to be a spicy, red, hot sun wine from the south, such as an Aglianico or a Primitivo.

Serves 8–10

1¾oz (40g) dried porcini mushrooms
1 large onion, finely chopped
¼ stick (40g) unsalted butter
1lb (500g) coarsely ground pork
7oz (200g) Italian sausage, casings removed and crumbled
3 tbsp concentrated tomato paste
1¼ cups (300ml) vegetable or chicken stock, warm
a pinch of freshly grated nutmeg
4 pints (2.5 liters) water
1 tbsp olive oil
1 tbsp coarse sea salt
3 cups (500g) polenta
¾ cup (75g) freshly grated Parmesan cheese
sea salt and freshly ground black pepper

Make the ragù first. In fact, you can do this up to 2 days ahead, and ragù always tastes best when it's been left to stand for a couple of days.

Cover the mushrooms with warm water and leave to stand for about 30 minutes.

Meanwhile, fry the onion gently in the butter in a large skillet for about 8 minutes, until softened. Add the ground pork and the sausage and fry together until browned, then stir in the tomato purée and stock. Strain the mushrooms through a piece of cheesecloth or a double layer of paper towels, then stir the mushrooms and the strained liquid into the ragù mixture. Add the nutmeg and season with salt and pepper to taste, then simmer over very low heat for about an hour, stirring occasionally. Keep the pan half-covered.

Bring the water to a rolling boil in a large saucepan and add the oil and the coarse sea salt. Trickle in the polenta, stirring constantly, and continue to stir for about 50 minutes, until the polenta is cooked and begins to come away from the side of the pan.

Spread a layer of hot ragù in a lightly oiled ovenproof serving dish, then add a layer of polenta and top with some Parmesan cheese. Continue layering until all the ingredients are used, ending with a layer of Parmesan. Place the dish in a preheated oven, 400°F, and bake for about 15 minutes until it is heated through and the top is golden. Serve at once.

Spezzatino di Maiale al Latte con le Fave
Pork Stewed in Milk with Fava Beans

In Puglia, the flat, brown fava bean is on sale everywhere, and is used extensively in all sorts of recipes from soups to pastries. These beans have a flavor that is completely different from that of a fresh British broad bean, utterly delicious, deeply nutty, and quite unique. I have found them in good Italian delicatessens outside of Puglia. Alternatively, you could use dried butter beans or chickpeas.

Serves 4

7oz (200g), about 1¼ cups dried brown fava beans, soaked overnight in cold water

¼ stick (25g) unsalted butter

2 tbsp extra virgin olive oil

1 onion, coarsely chopped

1 celery stalk, coarsely chopped

1 carrot, peeled and coarsely chopped

1 sprig fresh rosemary

1¾lb (875g) bone-in pork shoulder, skin removed, boned, and cut into 2-bite chunks

1 tbsp all-purpose white flour

1¾ cups (450ml) milk

about 1 cup (250ml) chicken or pork stock, warm

sea salt and freshly ground black pepper

1 handful fresh flat-leaf parsley, finely chopped

Drain the soaked fava beans and rinse thoroughly in cold running water. Place them in a saucepan, cover with fresh water, and bring to a boil, then boil hard for about 5 minutes. Drain and rinse the beans again, then set aside.

Meanwhile, melt the butter with the oil in a flameproof casserole. Add the onion, celery, carrot, and rosemary and fry, stirring occasionally, until the vegetables are softened. Add the chunks of meat and turn them in the hot fat and the vegetables for about 10 minutes, until browned all over. Sprinkle over the flour, stir together, and then add all the milk and salt and pepper to taste.

Cover the casserole tightly and simmer very slowly for about 30 minutes, occasionally adding a little stock if the stew appears to be drying out too quickly. After 30 minutes, stir in the drained fava beans and continue to cook until they are completely softened, about 30 minutes longer. When the meat is tender, take the stew off the heat, taste and adjust the seasoning. Sprinkle with the parsley to serve.

Gnocchi con le Polpettine
Gnocchi with Mini Meatballs

Sorry, but this is one of those occasions when timing is crucial for the success of the dish to be in any way guaranteed! It is typical of the kind of Italian kitchen that I love best, when the women of the household gather leisurely just to cook a great family favorite together. Each of them moving with such assured confidence around the table, never once ceasing the chatter and the good-humored gossip about each and every family member, be they be present or not. If there is only you, however, make sure everything is hot, or at the very least warm, when you combine all the different elements together, so don't be tempted to cook the meatballs or the sauce too far ahead of boiling the gnocchi. If your gnocchi are as light and tender as they should be, it will hard to mix the sauce and gnocchi together without some damage to the gnocchi, so try to use two spoons to mix them gently.

Serves 6

sea salt and freshly ground black pepper

freshly grated Parmesan or pecorino cheese
to serve

For the rich tomato sauce:

3–5 tbsp rich extra virgin olive oil

2 garlic cloves, thinly sliced or crushed

½ onion, finely chopped

1 celery stalk, finely chopped

1 carrot, peeled and finely chopped

2 tbsp finely chopped fresh flat-leaf parsley

1 heaping tbsp tomato paste

13oz (400g) canned tomatoes or passata
(crushed tomatoes)

1 tbsp unsalted butter

For the meatballs:

400g (13oz) ground veal, beef, turkey,
or chicken

2 cups (100g) fresh breadcrumbs

1 cup (100g) freshly grated Parmesan cheese

1 egg, beaten

3 tbsp chopped fresh flat-leaf parsley

½ wine glass cold water

freshly squeezed juice of ½ lemon

finely grated zest of 1 lemon

2 eggs, beaten

5 tbsp dry breadcrumbs

sunflower oil for deep-frying

(Continued...)

To make the tomato sauce, put the oil in a large, heavy-bottomed saucepan or skillet over medium heat with the garlic, onion, celery, carrot, and parsley and fry, stirring often, until all the vegetables are softened. Thoroughly stir in the tomato paste, then stir in the tomatoes and their juice. Cover the pan and simmer for about 40 minutes until the sauce is glossy and thick. Season to taste with salt and pepper.

Remove the pan from the heat. If you are going to use the sauce at once, stir in the butter. If, however, you are making the sauce in advance, do not add the butter until after you have reheated the sauce. (You can make this sauce up to 2 days in advance and store, covered, in the refrigerator.)

To make the meatballs, mix the meat, fresh breadcrumbs, Parmesan, beaten egg, parsley, and seasoning together thoroughly, and then blend in the water gradually. Finally, add the lemon juice and zest and use your hands to mix all the ingredients together. Shape the mixture into about 20 small balls about the size of a cherry.

Place the 2 beaten eggs in a dish and the dry breadcrumbs in another dish. Roll the meatballs in the beaten egg, then in the breadcrumbs until coated all over.

Heat enough oil for deep-frying in a heavy-bottomed saucepan or deep-fat fryer until it reaches 350–375°F/180–190°C, or a cube of bread browns in 30 seconds. Working in batches, add the meatballs and fry, stirring frequently, for about 4 minutes until they are crisp and browned. Remove them from the oil with a slotted spoon and drain thoroughly on paper towels. Set aside and keep them warm, uncovered, until required.

To make the gnocchi, boil the potatoes until soft, then drain and peel quickly. Press the potatoes through a potato ricer twice and put in a large bowl. Blend in the eggs and flour, adding as little flour as you can get away with, constantly testing the texture as you go along, until the dough can hold the gnocchi shape without collapsing. Work carefully and quickly, because the more you handle the dough, the harder and bouncier the gnocchi will become!

For the gnocchi:

2lb (1kg) floury potatoes, such as Yukon Gold, scrubbed

3 eggs, beaten

about 2½ cups (300g) all-purpose white flour, depending upon the texture of the potatoes

butter for greasing the dish

Make a soft dough ball in your hands out of the potato mixture, then cut into sections [1] and roll into long, thumb-thick cylinders. Cut these into cherry-size pieces [2] and form into about 90 small, concave gnocchi shapes, pressing them oh-so-gently against the back of a fork [3]. Leave them all spread out on a large board until required.

Bring a large pan of salted water to a gentle boil. Drop in the gnocchi, in very small batches, and allow them to cook until they float on the surface. Unless your gnocchi are of gigantic size or the water too cool, the gnocchi should take no more than 1 minute each to bob merrily to the top.

As the gnocchi are cooked, scoop them out with a slotted spoon and arrange them in shallow, lightly buttered serving dish. (It is easiest to dress the gnocchi without damaging them if they are in a shallow dish rather than in a deep bowl.) Reheat the tomato sauce and stir in the butter, if necessary, then spoon it and all the warm meatballs over the gnocchi. Give the dish a shake to help distribute the sauce and serve at once. Offer freshly grated Parmesan or pecorino separately at the table.

Bollito Misto
Boiled Meats

Believe it or not, this is one of Italy's great celebratory dishes, served on special occasions. In the end, however, it is nothing more than a combination of all kinds of meat, boiled together with vegetables until soft and delicious. Of course, the secret lies in starting with really high-quality ingredients, so their flavors stand out even after hours of simmering. It is important to serve various sauces, such as the *salsa verde* below, but also the ubiquitous accompaniment, *mostarda di cremona*, which consists of candied fruits preserved in a heavy mustard syrup. (Look for jars of it in good Italian delicatessens.) The idea of serving sauces that have a sweet-and-sour or piquant quality with the meats is to help enliven the various distinctive flavors. *Cotechino* is a traditional, fat rounded pork sausage with a very gutsy, full flavor.

Serves 8

1 cotechino, about 1lb 3oz (600g)
1 tongue, ready to cook
1 boiling fowl
1½lb (750g) veal breast
1½lb (750g) veal boneless rump roast
1½lb (750g) beef shank, or skirt
2 large onions
8 cloves
2 large carrots, peeled
3 celery stalks
8 black peppercorns
2 bay leaves
sea salt and freshly ground black pepper

For the salsa verde:
2 handfuls soft white breadcrumbs
4 tbsp white wine
4 tbsp white wine vinegar
2 garlic cloves
1 large handful fresh flat-leaf parsley leaves
2 whole salted anchovies, boned and thoroughly rinsed and dried
4 sour pickled gherkins (cornichons)
1 cup (250ml) extra virgin olive oil

To serve:
mostarda di cremona
various mustards

Pierce the cotechino all over with the point of a knife. Cover it with cold water and leave it to soak for about an hour, then drain. Return it to the rinsed saucepan, cover with fresh water and bring to a boil, then reduce the heat and simmer, uncovered, for 3 hours, skimming the surface occasionally.

Meanwhile, place the tongue in a separate pan with cold water to cover, and bring to a boil. Reduce the heat and simmer, uncovered, for 2 hours, skimming occasionally.

Place the boiling fowl in a third large pan and cover with cold water. Add one of the onions stuck with 4 of the cloves, 1 carrot, 1 celery stalk, 4 peppercorns, 1 bay leaf and salt to taste. Bring to a boil, then reduce the heat and simmer gently for 3 hours, skimming occasionally.

Place the veal breast, veal rump roast and the beef shank in a fourth pot with the remaining onion, carrot, celery, peppercorns, cloves, bay leaf, and salt to taste. Cover with cold water and bring to a boil, then reduce the heat and simmer for 3 hours, skimming occasionally.

Meanwhile, to make the salsa verde, put the breadcrumbs in a bowl. Mix the wine and vinegar together and pour over the breadcrumbs and leave to stand for 10 minutes. While the breadcrumbs are softening, put the garlic and parsley in a food processor or blender and whiz until puréed. Add the anchovy fillets and gherkins then whiz again.

Add the soaked breadcrumbs to the food processor and whiz again. With the motor running, drizzle in the olive oil until the sauce has a texture between pesto sauce and mint sauce. Season with salt and pepper to taste, then set aside until required.

When all the meat is cooked, transfer it all into a single pot, discarding all the excess liquid. Serve from the pot, taking out the various elements and carving them at the table on a large board. Each serving should contain a little bit of each type of meat and a slice each of carrot and celery for color. Serve piping hot with *salsa verde, mostarda di Cremona,* and various mustards.

Baked Rice Mold with Ragù

This is one of those really old-fashioned recipes, in which lots of saucepans are used to create a whole pile of washing up! But without the staff that existed to do the washing up in the days when the recipe was created, you can, perhaps, ask your guests to help. What I really like though, is that you can make the dish over several days, just making one section of the recipe at a time.

Serves 6

1oz (25g) dried porcini mushrooms
2 sticks (250g) unsalted butter, plus extra for greasing the mold
150g (5oz) ground veal or beef
2 small onions, finely chopped
1 celery stalk, finely chopped
3oz (75g) prosciutto crudo, ideally Parma ham, in 1 thick slice, diced
1 heaping tbsp tomato paste
½ cup (125ml) dry white wine
2 cups (250g) shelled peas
3 tbsp all-purpose white flour
½ cup (125ml) milk
2½ cups (450g) long-grain rice
1 cup (100g) freshly grated Parmesan cheese
8 leaves fresh basil, torn into small shreds with your fingers
3 tbsp chopped fresh flat-leaf parsley
2 eggs, beaten
5 tbsp dried breadcrumbs for lining the mold
sea salt and freshly ground black pepper
rich tomato sauce (see page 109) to serve (optional)

Cover the mushrooms generously in boiling water and leave them to stand for about 45 minutes, and then drain them through cheesecloth or a double layer of paper towels, reserving the liquid. Strain the water through cheesecloth or paper towels again and set aside.

Melt about 1 tbsp (15g) of the butter in a saucepan. Add the mushrooms and fry gently, stirring occasionally and adding the strained water gradually as required, for about 20 minutes. When the mushrooms are completely softened, chop them finely and set aside; reserve any remaining liquid.

Meanwhile, melt 3½oz (100g) of butter in a separate pan over low heat. Add the ground meat, half the onion, the celery, half the ham, and the tomato paste, stirring frequently and gradually adding the wine. When the meat is browned all over and the onion is soft and transparent, season to taste and add the chopped mushrooms and half of their remaining liquid; set aside.

In a separate saucepan, melt 1½oz (40g) of the remaining butter with the remaining onion and ham until the onion is transparent and shiny. Add the peas, season to taste, and stew them gently until soft, stirring frequently and adding warm stock as required. When the peas are soft, add them to the ground meat mixture and continue to simmer very gently.

Now make a thick béchamel sauce by melting 2oz (50g) of the butter in a small saucepan until foaming. Stir in the flour until you have a smooth paste. Stir in the milk and the reserved mushroom soaking liquid, then simmer very slowly, stirring constantly, until the sauce has thickened.

Add the sauce to the ground meat and pea mixture and stir very thoroughly. Taste and adjust seasoning accordingly; set aside.

Meanwhile, bring a large pan of water to a boil. Add the rice and boil for about 10 minutes until just tender. Drain the rice and rinse it thoroughly under cold running water, then shake off any excess water and put in a large bowl.

Melt the rest of the butter, then pour it over the rice and mix in thoroughly with 2 forks. Add the Parmesan, basil, parsley, and eggs and season to taste.

Butter an 8-in (20-cm) ring mold and sprinkle half the breadcrumbs generously all over the inside to line it completely. Turn the mold upside down and shake to remove any excess breadcrumbs and discard them. Put half the rice in the mold, pressing it down firmly with a spatula or the back of a spoon. Cover with all the sauce, press down, then cover with the rest of the rice and press down again to force it all in the mold. Bang the mold firmly on the work surface to settle the grains. Dot the top with the remaining butter and sprinkle with the remaining breadcrumbs.

Place the mold in a preheated oven, 375°F, and bake for about 30 minutes, until the top is golden and crunchy. Remove from the oven and leave to rest for 8 minutes, then carefully invert on to a serving plate and remove the mold. If you like, you can offer round a sauceboat of rich tomato sauce for guests to pour over their portion.

Pere al Forno con Prosciutto e Fontina

Wrapped Pears

Serve this beautiful dish either as an appetizer or as a savory end to a dinner, whichever way round works best for you. This is truly scrumptious, but make sure the pears are just at the right point of ripeness, not rock hard but definitely not mushy either.

Serves 4
6 black peppercorns
2 bay leaves
2 cups (500ml) dry white wine
4 cups (1 liter) water
4 pears, peeled and left whole including their stalks and cores
freshly squeezed juice of ½ lemon
2oz (50g) fontina cheese, finely cubed
4 fresh sage leaves, finely chopped
1 sprig fresh thyme, leaves removed and finely chopped
8 paper-thin slices Parma ham

Place the peppercorns, bay leaves, wine, and water in a deep saucepan large enough to hold the pears upright. Brush the pears all over with the lemon juice, then carefully stand them upright in the pan and place it over a medium heat. Cover the pan and bring the liquid to a boil, then reduce the heat and simmer for 30 minutes or until the pears are soft but still firm. Remove from the liquid and allow them to drain and cool. Slice the bottom off each pear carefully and reserve the removed slice.

Mix the fontina with the herbs. Using an apple corer, carefully remove the core from each pear from the underside and discard. Fill the resulting cavity with the cheese and herbs. Replace the removed slice of pear and wrap each filled pear in 2 slices of Parma ham.

Stand each wrapped and filled pear on a sheet of nonstick baking parchment in a roasting pan. Place the pan in a preheated oven, 425°F, and bake for about 20 minutes or until the ham becomes crispy. Remove the pears from the oven and leave to rest for about 5 minutes before serving.

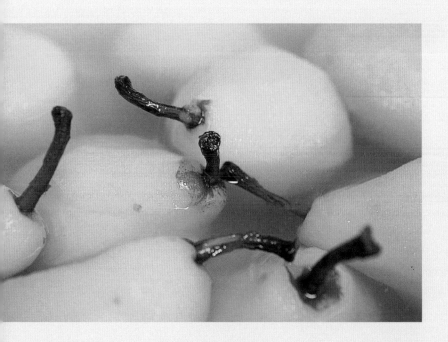

Rotolo di Pasta con Ricotta e Spinaci

Pasta Roll with Ricotta and Spinach

You will need a very wide saucepan or a fish kettle to cook this. It's a little laborious in terms of having to make the pasta and rolling it out by hand, but otherwise is a very simple recipe and an interesting and different take on a pasta theme. You can vary the fillings once you have mastered the knack.

Serves 6

sea salt and freshly ground black pepper
½ cup (40g) freshly grated Parmesan
cheese, to serve

For the filling:
2lb (1kg) fresh spinach, picked over and
rinsed in several changes of water
7oz (200g) fresh ricotta
1 egg, beaten
pinch of freshly grated nutmeg
1½ cups (175g) freshly grated Parmesan
cheese

For the pasta:
about 3½ cups (500g) all-purpose
white flour
5 eggs

For the sage butter:
1 handful fresh sage leaves, rinsed
and dried
3 tbsp sunflower oil
1¼ sticks (150g) unsalted butter

Make the pasta, using the flour and eggs and following the instructions on page 57. Shape into a ball, wrap in plastic wrap and leave to rest for 20 minutes.

Meanwhile, place the spinach in a large saucepan over medium-high heat with just the water clinging to the leaves and steam just until wilted and tender; drain and leave to cool. When cool enough to handle, squeeze the spinach between your hands until it feels reasonably dry, then chop finely. Place the spinach in a bowl, add the ricotta, egg, nutmeg, Parmesan, and salt and pepper to taste and mix together; set aside.

Roll out the pasta by hand, following the instructions on page 57, into a wide, thin sheet, about the size of a small tea towel. Spread the spinach filling over the pasta to within 1¼in (3cm) of the edge, then roll up tightly from one of the short ends, as if making a jelly roll, making sure there is no air between each turn of the spiral.

Wrap the pasta roll tightly in a piece of clean cheesecloth. Tie the ends tightly with kitchen string, leaving a secure loop so you can lift it easily out of the water once it is cooked. Bring a fish kettle of salted water to a boil. Slide the wrapped roll into the water carefully and boil gently for about 45 minutes. The only tricky bit is keeping the roll straight as it cooks, so it is important not to let it sag in the center.

While the pasta roll is cooking, make the sage butter. Divide the sage leaves into two piles, one slightly larger than the other and made up of larger leaves. Melt the butter very slowly in a very small, heavy-bottomed saucepan. Rub the smaller pile of leavers gently in your palms to release the essential oils and drop them into the melting butter. Swirl the pan occasionally but never be tempted to stir the butter. Keep a close eye on the butter as you don't want it to burn. If it browns, it will take on a new flavor and mask the sage, and you should throw it away and start again.

In a separate small skillet, heat the sunflower oil until sizzling hot. Drop the sage leaves into the oil to sizzle for seconds, no more than a minute, turning the leaves so they don't burn. The leaves are ready when they curl up and become crisp and slightly translucent. Drain them thoroughly on paper towels, sprinkle with salt, and put to one side until required: do not cover them or they will become soggy and bitter.

Carefully remove the pasta roll from the water and drain by holding the cloth firmly with tongs at each end and leave to drip dry. Unwrap very slowly and carefully and lay it on a board, then cut into 12 neat slices with a very sharp knife. Arrange the slices on a waiting warmed platter and spoon over the sage butter. Sprinkle with the fried leaves and the freshly grated Parmesan and serve at once.

Tontino di Riso con Radicchio

Rice "Pancake" with Radicchio

I love this kind of rice dish. It makes a good appetizer before a meat or fish main course when you are not in the mood for soup, pasta, or a creamy risotto. This is also a very good vegetarian standby dish. Do not be tempted to stint on the amount of time you allow the *tortino* to cook on each side or the whole thing really will fall to pieces as you cut it.

Serves 6

¼ stick (25g) unsalted butter
1 large shallot, finely chopped
2 heads of radicchio, rinsed and coarsely chopped
4 tbsp olive oil
7oz (200g) fontina or Gruyère cheese, rind removed if necessary and cut into thin strips
sea salt and freshly ground black pepper

For the cheese risotto:
1 onion, finely chopped
¾ stick (75g) unsalted butter
2 cups (400g) risotto rice
about 2½ pints (1.5 litres) best-quality chicken or meat stock, or very strongly flavored vegetable stock, kept hot
¾ cup (75g) freshly grated Parmesan cheese

Begin by making the risotto. Fry the onion in half the butter for about 10 minutes over very low heat or until the onion is soft but not colored. Stir in the rice and toast the grains on all sides, stirring constantly, for about 5 minutes. Add the first 2 or 3 ladles of hot stock and stir until all the liquid is absorbed. Continue adding the stock, one ladleful at a time, letting the rice absorb the liquid at its own pace and stirring constantly. The rice will tell you when its time to add more stock by opening up a clear wake through the grains behind the spoon as you draw it through the cooking risotto.

When the rice is soft and creamy, stir in the cheese and the rest of the butter. Taste and adjust seasoning, then cover and leave to rest for about 3 minutes before tipping out on to a shallow tray to cool completely.

While the risotto is cooling, make the *tortino*. Melt the butter in a saucepan over medium heat. Add the shallot and the radicchio and cook until the shallot is tender and the radicchio wilts. Stir in salt and pepper to taste, then set aside.

Heat a large, nonstick skillet with 2 tablespoons of the olive oil over high heat. When the oil is very hot, take the skillet off the heat and cover the base with half the cold risotto, using a spatula to flatten it into a thick pancake. Return the skillet to a medium heat and cover the risotto layer with the radicchio and the fontina, patting them down firmly. Spread over the remaining risotto in an even layer. Cook for about 10 minutes, shaking the skillet occasionally to prevent burning.

Carefully invert the pancake on to a wide platter. Wipe any debris from the skillet, then pour in the remaining 2 tablespoons oil. Heat for 2 minutes or so over high heat, then reduce the heat to medium and slide the rice pancake carefully back in, cooked side up. Cook for a further 10 minutes as before, then slide out on to a platter and leave to cool for 5 minutes. Slice into wedges to serve.

5 *pleasurable puddings*

And so to our final chapter of sweet indulgences, among which, as the title would suggest, there are quite a few puddings, which in Italian are called *budino* in the singular, and *budini* in the plural. The idea of a soft, gentle dessert into which the spoon can sink smoothly is both comforting and luscious, and to my mind we all need as much of that kind of thing as possible! Of particular interest to all the chocoholics among you is the delicious classic *Budino al Cioccolato* on page 124, which needs the very best dark, rich chocolate to make it into a thing of truly sumptuous perfection. The Italian menu does not usually contain very many desserts. We prefer to end our meals with fruit or some hard *biscotti* to dunk into a glass of amber colored sweet wine, or perhaps an ice cream, and definitely a tiny cup of espresso, but I have assembled as many as I could for you in this final chapter, so as to end this book on the sweetest of notes.

Dolce di Cigliege
Cherry Cake

This is a classic baked ricotta cake with dark cherries mixed through. Don't be surprised if the cherries sink to the bottom. This is fine and absolutely in keeping with the nature of this very soft textured cake.

Serves 6–8

1 walnut-sized piece of butter for greasing

10oz (300g) very fresh ricotta or cream cheese

1⅓ cups (300g) granulated or superfine sugar

3 eggs, separated

4 tbsp milk

¾ cup (75g) finest possible cake flour, sifted twice

finely grated rind of 1 large lemon

1 tbsp baking powder

10oz (300g) ripe black cherries, pitted and halved

4 tbsp confectioners' sugar

cream, whipped mascarpone, or ice cream to serve

Line a 8-in (20-cm) springform cake pan with baking parchment, then grease very generously with butter; set aside.

If you are using cream cheese instead of ricotta, whip it with a balloon whisk first to lighten it. Replace the whisk with an electric mixer and continue to beat the whipped cream cheese or ricotta lightly for 10–15 minutes, gradually adding the sugar, until the mixture appears light and fluffy. Beat the egg yolks with the milk, then gradually whisk this into the cheese mixture, followed by the flour, lemon rind, and baking powder. Finally, gently fold the cherries though the mixture. Put the chilled egg whites into a clean bowl and use clean and dry beaters to beat them until stiff peaks form, then carefully fold them into the cake mixture.

Pour the mixture into the prepared pan and level the surface smoothly with the back of a spoon. Place in a preheated oven, 325°F, and bake for 45–60 minutes, until a long, thin metal skewer pushed deep into the center of the cake comes out perfectly clean. Do not worry if the middle of the cake sinks a little, this is quite normal, as this is a very soft cake that is much more like a firm pudding than a conventional cake.

Remove the pan from the oven and leave the cake to cool for about 10 minutes before unmolding and sliding the cake on to a wire rack to cool completely. Sift the confectioners' sugar all over the cake and serve warm, with cream, whipped mascarpone, or ice cream.

Peach Cake

This lovely moist cake is perfect on its own, but also delicious with cream or warm custard sauce. I also think it is wonderful made with apples, pears, plums, or apricots.

Serves 6

¼ cup + 1 tbsp (65g) butter, cut into small pieces, plus extra for greasing
3 tbsp stale breadcrumbs
3 large eggs
⅔ cup (150g) superfine sugar
2 cups (200g) all-purpose white flour, sifted
⅔ cup (150ml) milk
finely grated rind of ½ lemon
1 heaping tsp baking powder, sifted
2lb (1kg) peaches, pitted and sliced
2 tbsp granulated or light brown sugar

Butter a 10-in (5-cm) springform cake pan generously with butter, then dust with the breadcrumbs. Turn the pan upside-down to remove the loose breadcrumbs and discard them; set the tin aside.

Place the eggs in a bowl and beat until light and fluffy, adding the sugar gradually, then fold in the flour, milk, lemon rind, and baking powder: the mixture should be quite liquid. Add half the sliced peaches to the cake mixture and stir through.

Pour the cake mixture into the prepared pan, arrange the remaining sliced peaches on the top, dot with the butter and sprinkle with the sugar. Place the cake pan in a preheated oven, 350°F, and bake for 55 minutes, until a knife pushed into the center comes out clean and dry.

Remove the cake from the oven and leave to cool completely on a wire rack before removing from the pan and cutting into wedges.

Castagnaccio

Rustic Chestnut Flour Cake

This is an incredibly simple Tuscan recipe that uses a few basic ingredients that were once indigenous to the area. The texture varies according to whether you make a thick version in a deep cake pan, or you make it pancake thin in a wider, shallow baking sheet. It is delicious warm, spread with mildly sour stracchino cheese or sweet, fresh ricotta. Chestnut flour isn't an everyday ingredient but is available in the winter in some Italian delicatessens.

Serves 6

¾ cup (75g) golden raisins
5–6 tbsp extra virgin olive oil
1lb (500g) chestnut flour
6 tbsp (75g) superfine sugar
pinch of salt
about 4 cups (1 liter) cold water
2 tbsp rosemary leaves or fennel seeds
½ cup (50g) pine nuts

Cover the golden raisins with warm water and leave to soak for 15 minutes, then drain and dry them with care. Grease a baking pan thoroughly with olive oil. The size of the baking pan will depend upon whether you like the idea of your *castagnaccio* being deep and thick, or thinner and less stodgy. This is entirely a personal preference, bearing in mind the *castagnaccio* will not rise at all.

Mix the chestnut flour, sugar, and salt together, then add about 3 tablespoons olive oil, beating constantly. Gradually add the cold water to make a thick, lump-free batter. Pour the batter into the pan and level the surface. Sprinkle with the rosemary or fennel, the golden raisins and the pine nuts. Place the baking pan in the preheated oven, 375°F, and bake for 45–60 minutes, depending upon how dry or wet you like it. Leave to cool slightly, then serve warm or at room temperature.

Zuppa Inglese
Italian Trifle

This is absolutely nothing like an English trifle, but very delicious nevertheless—I often wonder which came first, the English or the Neapolitan version! What is amusing is the name—translated literally, it means English soup—which has never struck me as being terribly complimentary! You can make this a day in advance and keep it in the refrigerator until needed, if you like.

Serves 6–8
10 tbsp dark rum
10 tbsp of your favorite liqueur
1lb 2oz (550g) fresh ricotta
4oz (125g) best quality Continental dark chocolate (at least 70% cocoa), grated
⅔ cup (150g) sugar
2 tsp vanilla extract
2 tbsp cold water
1–2 packets ladyfingers

Mix the rum and liqueur in a bowl and pour half of the mixture into a second bowl. Sieve the ricotta into one of the bowls and stir until thoroughly mixed. Stir in about one-third of the chocolate.

Put the sugar, vanilla, and water into a small saucepan and melt together until a smooth caramel syrup forms (see Caramel-making tips, below). Allow the syrup to cool to hand heat, then pour into the ricotta mixture gradually, stirring constantly.

Dip the ladyfingers into the remaining rum and liqueur mixture, then arrange a layer in the bottom of a pretty bowl. Pour over a layer of the ricotta mixture, and then cover with another layer of dipped ladyfingers. Continue until all the ladyfingers and the ricotta mixture have been used, finishing with a layer of ricotta mixture. Sprinkle over the remaining grated chocolate and chill for at least an hour before serving.

Caramel-making tips:
There are various stages of caramel, from the palest yellow to the darkest, burnt-sugar brown. At each stage the flavor of the caramel intensifies. In all cases, the secret is never to give in to the temptation to stir the melting sugar. Swirl the pan gently, taking great care not to splash your skin with the caramel as it will stick to you and burn terribly. The swirling action should be enough to mix up the sugar and water and thus caramelize it evenly. Never abandon your caramel while it is cooking, but watch it carefully to be sure it doesn't burn or cook unevenly.

La Cassata alla Siciliana a modo
Sicilian Cassata Revisited

This amazingly rich and sumptuous Sicilian classic was traditionally made in the springtime, when milk was abundant and there was plenty available for cheese-making. It has its origins buried deep in Sicily's culinary history, taking its name from the Arab word meaning "big round bowl." Buy some good quality, ready-made fondant frosting and knead in a few drops of natural green food coloring to turn it a pale green.

Serves 8

1lb (500g) fresh ricotta
3 cups (300g) confectioners' sugar, sifted
1 tsp vanilla extract
3 tbsp rum or sticky liqueur of your choice
1¾oz (40g) best quality Continental dark chocolate, chopped
3 tbsp chopped mixed candied peel
10oz (300g) plain sponge cake, thinly sliced
6 tbsp prepared custard sauce
(see page 138)

To decorate:
pale green fondant frosting
flakes of chocolate, candied fruit, glacé fruit, silver balls, sprinkles, rice-paper flowers, colored dragees and so on

Push the ricotta through a sieve to make it really smooth, then beat it lightly with the confectioners' sugar until it is has the consistency of lightly whipped cream. Flavor the ricotta mixture with the vanilla and rum or liqueur. Gently mix in the chocolate and candied peel with a light touch to prevent knocking all the air out.

Line a 16-in (5-cm) bowl or pudding basin smoothly with plastic wrap, pulling it tight to prevent creases, then line it with the slices of cake, using the custard to "cement" the slices together securely and to stick the cake into position. Spoon in the ricotta mixture, gently smoothing the top. Put a plate on the top and press it down, then place the bowl in the refrigerator for 2–3 hours.

When you're ready to serve, invert the cassata on to a plate, remove the bowl and carefully peel off the plastic wrap. Lightly dust the work surface with confectioners' sugar and roll out the fondant frosting until it is about ¼in (0.5mm) thick and even all over. Thickly cover the cassata with the soft fondant frosting. Use a palette knife dipped into hot water to smooth the surface perfectly. Add whatever decorations you like, then chill the cassata, uncovered, until required, but eat within 24 hours.

Budino al Cioccolato
Classic Chocolate Pudding

When my family comes to visit, this is the alternative, child-friendly pudding I give my four step-granddaughters.

Serves 4

1¾oz (40g) best quality Continental dark chocolate
1¾ cups (400ml) milk
1 tsp vanilla extract
2 eggs
4 tbsp superfine sugar
1 tbsp cornstarch, sifted

Melt the chocolate in a bowl set over a pan of simmering water with 3½fl oz (100ml) of the milk, stirring until smooth and blended. Remove the pan from the heat and stir in the remaining milk and the vanilla. Return the pan to the heat and stir gently until the mixture reaches a boil, then take off the heat again and leave to cool. Beat the eggs with the sugar, then stir them in to the cool chocolate mixture with the cornstarch.

Pour the chocolate mixture into a dampened 17-fl oz (500-ml) mold, then place in a roasting pan with enough cold water to come two-thirds of the way up the side of the mold. Place the roasting pan in the preheated oven, 350°F, and bake for 30–40 minutes until set.

Leave the pudding to cool completely, then cover and chill for at least an hour. Invert the pudding onto a serving plate and remove the mold. Serve at once.

Budini di Mandorle Noci e Caramello

Caramel, Walnut, and Almond Puddings

Very pretty to look at, these lovely little warm puddings are a perfect end to any special lunch or dinner. You can really go to town with the caramel in terms of decorating, provided you are really careful not to let it touch you, as a sugar burn is always horribly painful.

Serves 8

1 stick (100g) unsalted butter, plus a little extra for buttering the ramekins or molds

⅔ cup (75g) all-purpose flour

1 cup (225g) superfine sugar

¾ cup (200ml) milk

3 tbsp cold water

½ cup (100ml) light cream

2 whole eggs

2 egg yolks

1 egg white

pinch of sea salt

butter for greasing

8 shelled walnuts

16 blanched almonds

Butter eight 4-fl oz (125-ml) ramekins or dariole molds thoroughly; set aside. Melt 3oz (75g) of the butter in a small saucepan over medium heat. Stir in the flour, 5½ tablespoons of the sugar, and the milk, stirring over a very low heat until a thick, smooth sauce forms; set aside and leave to cool.

In a separate pan, melt 7 tablespoons of the sugar with 2 tablespoons of the water to make a smooth, golden-brown caramel (see Caramel-making tips, page 123). While the caramel is bubbling, warm the cream to just below boiling point in a separate pan. As soon as the caramel is golden brown, take the pan off the heat and add the cream, stirring until blended, then set aside to cool for a few minutes.

When the caramel cream is cool, mix it into the thick butter sauce. Blend in the eggs and egg yolks. Whisk the egg white until frothy, then add the salt and whisk until stiff peaks form. Use a large metal spoon or rubber spatula to fold into the cream mixture.

Divide the mixture between the prepared ramekins or molds, then place them in a roasting pan with enough water to come two-thirds of the way up the sides. Place the pan in a preheated oven, 350°F, and bake for 40–45 minutes, until the puddings are set. Turn off the heat, leave the oven door ajar, and let the puddings cool.

To serve, place the remaining sugar in a small pan with the remaining tablespoon of water and make a golden brown caramel as above. When the caramel is smooth and golden brown, remove the pan from the heat, add the nuts and swirl the pan to distribute them evenly; set aside until the caramel is tacky.

Invert the puddings on to 8 plates, run a spatula around the edges and then lift off the containers. Draw the nuts out of the caramel and distribute them evenly on top of the puddings to garnish. Serve at once.

Amaretto and Pear Puddings with Zabaglione

What I love about this dessert is the balance of all the flavors. The amaretto and the zabaglione are just enough to make it appear really grown up and add a touch of sophistication. I like to use Williams pears (if available) for this recipe.

Serves 6

1lb (500g) pears, peeled, cored, and quartered

1¾ cups (400ml) medium-dry white wine

½ cup (125g) superfine sugar

6 cloves

½ stick (50g) unsalted butter, plus extra for greasing

4 eggs, beaten

3oz (75g) amaretti cookies, crumbled

½ cup less 2 tbsp (70g) potato flour or cornstarch

For the zabaglione:

4 egg yolks

8 tbsp Marsala

4 tbsp superfine sugar

Butter six 4-fl oz (125-ml) ramekins or other ovenproof molds; set aside.

Place the pears in a saucepan with the wine, just under ½ the sugar and the cloves, stirring to dissolve the sugar. Bring to a simmer and continue to simmer, covered, for about 10 minutes or until the pears have softened. Take out 2 pear quarters and reserve. Drain the remaining pears, discard the cloves, place in a food processor or blender and whiz until smooth.

Return the pear purée to the pan and place over the heat again to dry it out a little, mixing in the butter. Remove the pan from the heat and leave to cool.

In a bowl, whisk the beaten eggs with the remaining sugar, then stir into the pear purée. Stir in the crumbled amaretti and the potato flour or cornflour. Divide this mixture between the prepared ramekins, then stand them in a roasting pan with enough cold water to come two-thirds of the way up the sides.

Place the roasting pan in a preheated oven, 350°F, for about 35 minutes or until set. Remove from the oven and set aside to cool completely.

Meanwhile, to make the zabaglione, mix all the ingredients together in a large heatproof bowl or saucepan set over another pan of very hot, but not boiling, water and beat for 10 minutes until the zabaglione is foamy, pale yellow, thick and shiny. Or, use a balloon whisk, which will take about 20 minutes. The zabaglione will separate as it cools, so don't make it too far ahead and keep it warm over the hot water, whisking occasionally. For tips on making zabaglione, see page 22.

When you are ready to serve, divide the zabaglione between 6 bowls. Invert and unmold the puddings and place one in the center of each bowl. Slice the reserved poached pear quarters, then divide them between the bowls.

Budino al Caffè con Panna
Coffee Dessert with Whipped Cream

A delightfully trembly, cool coffee dessert. Make sure this has really set firmly before you take it out of the oven, otherwise it can collapse when you unmold it.

Serves 6
butter for greasing
1¾ cups (450ml) milk
1 tbsp instant coffee granules
3½ tbsp (50ml) coffee-flavored liqueur
4 whole eggs
4 egg yolks
½ cup (125g) superfine sugar
1 tbsp unsweetened cocoa powder

To serve:
½ cup (100ml) whipping cream
1 tbsp confectioners' sugar, sifted
2oz (50g) bitter or bittersweet chocolate shavings
about 12 coffee beans

Butter a 1¼-pint (750-ml) ovenproof mold; set aside. Heat the milk until just boiling, then take the pan off the heat and stir in the instant coffee. Leave the milk to cool slightly, then stir in the liqueur.

Put the eggs, egg yolks, and superfine sugar in a bowl and beat with an electric mixer until they are pale and foaming, then sift in the cocoa powder. Gradually stir in the coffee and milk mixture.

Pour the mixture into the prepared mold, then place the mold in a roasting pan with enough cold water to come two-thirds of the way up the sides of the mold. Place the pan in a preheated oven, 350°F, and bake for 60 minutes or until firmly set.

Remove the mold from the oven and leave the dessert to cool to room temperature before refrigerating.

Meanwhile, whip the cream with the confectioners' sugar until thick and holding its shape. When you're ready to serve, run a spatula around the edge of the mold, turn the dessert onto a serving platter and remove the mold. Decorate with the whipped cream, the chocolate shavings, and the coffee beans. Serve at once.

Frittelle di Ricotta al Cioccolato

Ricotta and Chocolate Fritters

One of those very old-fashioned recipes from Italy's deep south. This is quite tricky to make without half the filling falling into the oil (which is very messy!) but delicious as long as you are careful to seal each fritter so you can finish with them intact, crisp, and perfect!

Makes about 36

sunflower oil for frying

For the dough:
4 cups (550g) all-purpose white flour
3 tbsp superfine sugar
3 tbsp unsweetened cocoa powder
about 1¼ cups (300ml) dry white wine
3½oz (100g) lard, or vegetable fat,
finely diced

For the filling:
1½lb (750g) fresh ricotta, well drained
1 cup (200g) sugar
100g (3½oz) best quality Continental dark
chocolate (at least 70% cocoa), grated,
or the finely grated rind of 2 lemons

To serve:
5 tbsp confectioners' sugar, sifted
1 tsp ground cinnamon

To make the dough, sift together the flour, sugar, and cocoa on to a marble or wooden surface. Make a well in the center and slowly pour the wine into the well, using as much as it takes to make a fairly solid, thick dough. Knead the lard, piece by piece, into the dough. When all the lard is incorporated, knead the dough for about 15 minutes, rolling the dough out into a long strip, then folding it back up on to itself, and rolling it out again. Incorporate as much air into the dough as possible, kneading until it is shiny and elastic, but not greasy. Put the dough into a bowl, cover with a cloth or a sheet of plastic wrap, and let it rest for at least an hour.

Meanwhile, make the filling. Sieve the ricotta into a bowl, then mix it thoroughly with the sugar, beating vigorously. Mix in the chocolate or the lemon rind.

Roll out the dough into a very thin sheet, on a floured surface to help prevent sticking. Cut into 2½-in (6-cm) circles with a greased cutter. On each circle place a scant tablespoonful of the ricotta mixture. Fold the disk over into a half moon, moisten the edge and press to seal securely.

Heat at least 4in (10cm) of oil in a large saucepan or deep fat fryer until a cube of bread browns after 30 seconds when it is dropped in. Add the filled fritters in batches and fry until they are golden brown and crisp. Remove with a slotted spoon and drain on paper towels. Continue until all the fritters are fried and serve warm, sprinkled with sifted confectioners' sugar and ground cinnamon.

Budino di Cioccolato e Vaniglia con Crema al Cocco

Marbled Chocolate and Vanilla Pudding with Coconut Cream Sauce

You can, of course, serve the pudding with a chocolate or vanilla custard sauce instead of coconut, though I think the coconut adds an interestingly exotic note.

Serves 6

1 stick (100g) unsalted butter
⅔ cup (75g) all-purpose white flour
2 cups (500ml) milk
4 whole eggs
2 egg yolks
⅔ cup (150g) superfine sugar
6 tbsp unsweetened cocoa powder
2 tsp vanilla essence
butter for greasing

For the coconut cream sauce:
1¾ cups (400ml) milk
⅖ cup (100ml) coconut cream
2 tbsp superfine sugar
2 egg yolks
1 tbsp all-purpose white flour
1 tsp ground cinnamon

Butter and line the base and sides of a 1¾-pint (1-litre) loaf pan; set aside.

Melt the butter in a small saucepan over medium-high heat. When it is hot and liquid, reduce the heat to low and stir in the flour, then the milk, whisking to remove any lumps and lower the heat under the pan to a minimum. Continue to cook this mixture slowly, stirring constantly until thick enough to come away from the sides of the pan. Take the pan off the heat and set aside to cool.

Beat the whole eggs with the yolks and the sugar until pale and foaming, then stir into the cooled milk mixture. Divide this mixture between two separate bowls. Add the cocoa powder to one bowl, and the vanilla to the other. Stir both mixtures until they are smooth and well blended.

Pour the contents of each bowl into the prepared tin in alternate layers so that one layer lies on top of the other. Draw a knife through the mixtures at this point to create the marble effect. Place the loaf pan in a roasting pan with enough cold water to come two-thirds up the sides. Place the pan in a preheated oven, 350°F, and bake for about 60 minutes or until set.

Meanwhile, to make the coconut cream sauce, pour the milk into a pan and bring to a boil. Remove the pan from the heat, add the coconut cream and stir together. Beat the egg yolks in a separate bowl with the sugar. Add the flour and the cinnamon and beat this into the milk and coconut cream. Put the saucepan back on the heat and bring back to a low boil, stirring constantly until thickened. Transfer the sauce to a bowl to cool, sprinkling the top with a little cold milk, or putting a piece of plastic wrap directly on the surface, to prevent a skin from forming.

When the pudding comes out of the oven, leave it to cool slightly, then turn out on to a board. Slice and serve, with the coconut cream sauce offered separately.

La Rocciata

Fruit and Nut Pastry Roll

This is a rustic cake, slightly similar to a strudel, but not nearly as refined. It is packed full of nuts and the distinctive flavor of aniseed. I find it really delicious served warm at the end of a meal with the vanilla sauce and a glass or two of dessert wine.

Serves 8
2 tbsp aniseed seeds
1 cup (250ml) boiling water

For the vanilla sauce:
2 cups (500ml) milk
1 vanilla bean, slit lengthways
5 egg yolks
½ cup (100g) superfine sugar
3 tbsp dark rum
small knob of cold unsalted butter

For the pastry:
2 cups (250g) all-purpose white flour,
plus extra for dusting
1½ tsp baking powder
5 tbsp sunflower or olive oil
3 tbsp aniseed-flavored liqueur or spirit,
such as Sambuca, Pernod, or Anisette
3 tbsp dark rum
1 tsp vanilla extract
pinch of salt

For the filling:
1 large pear
1 large dessert apple
½ cup (50g) golden raisins covered in warm
water and allowed to swell for 15 minutes
3 tbsp superfine sugar
3 tbsp unsweetened cocoa powder
4 tsp grappa
½ tsp ground cinnamon
finely grated rind of 1 unwaxed lemon
finely grated rind of 2 unwaxed oranges
1 cup (100g) shelled walnuts, chopped
4 tbsp dried breadcrumbs
4 tbsp apricot conserve, just warmed
1 tsp ground white pepper
sunflower oil for glazing

Cover the aniseed seeds with the hot water and leave to stand for about 10 minutes, then strain and reserve the softened seeds and the water.

Make the sauce next. Bring the milk to just below boiling point in a saucepan with the vanilla bean. Take the pan off the heat and set aside to cool and infuse. Beat the egg yolks vigorously in a bowl with the sugar until pale, then gradually add the strained milk, in a fine stream, whisking constantly. Pour back into the saucepan and place over a low heat, stirring gently until the sauce thickens enough to coat the back of a wooden spoon. Take the pan off the heat and stir in the rum. Rub a small knob of cold butter over the top of the sauce to prevent a skin forming; set aside.

Now, move on to the pastry. Sift the flour and baking powder on to the work surface and make a well in the center. Pour the oil, the aniseed spirit or liqueur and the rum into the center, then add the water in which the aniseeds were infused, the vanilla extract and salt. Knead all these ingredients together to form a smooth, shiny ball of dough. Cover the dough with an empty warmed saucepan and leave it to rest for about 30 minutes.

Meanwhile, to prepare the filling, peel, core and cube the pear and the apple. Drain and dry the golden raisins and add them to the apple and pear with the sugar, cocoa powder, grappa, cinnamon, reserved aniseed seeds, grated lemon and orange rinds, and the walnuts. Stir together thoroughly and leave to rest for 30 minutes.

Using a lightly floured rolling pin, roll out the pastry dough as thinly as possible on a floured surface. Carefully transfer it to a clean cloth larger than the rolled-out pastry and sprinkle with the breadcrumbs. Spread the filling mixture evenly over the pastry, leaving an uncovered rim about as wide as a thumb thickness around the edges. Mix the conserve with an equal amount of warm water, then spread this over the filling. Finally, sprinkle with the white pepper.

Using the cloth to help you, roll the *rocciata* tightly, as if rolling a jelly roll, and seal the ends securely by pinching tightly. Soak a large sheet of baking parchment in cold water, then squeeze dry and lay it on a baking sheet. Carefully transfer the *rocciata* to the baking parchment and gently twist the pastry into a ring, tucking under the ends. Brush lightly with the oil to glaze. Place the baking sheet in a preheated oven, 325°F, and bake for about 30 minutes, until golden brown. Serve warm or cold, with the warmed sauce served separately.

White Chocolate and Zabaglione Mousse

This is a great party piece, and is absolutely delicious with fresh raspberries, as you need the sharpness of the fruit to cut through the sweetness of the mousses. It looks especially spectacular served in wide martini cocktail-type glasses.

Serves 8

For the zabaglione:
4 egg yolks
4 tbsp superfine sugar
8 tbsp Marsala
2 sheets gelatin, or 2 tsp powdered gelatin
½ cup (125ml) whipping cream, lightly whipped

For the white chocolate mousse:
4 eggs, separated, whites chilled
4 tbsp superfine sugar
8½oz (225g) white chocolate, chopped
1 extra egg white, chilled

To serve:
amaretti biscuits, *langues de chat* or similar
1 handful fresh raspberries

To make the zabaglione, mix the egg yolks, sugar, and Marsala together in a large, heavy bowl or saucepan over a pan of simmering, but not boiling water. Whisk constantly with a balloon whisk until foaming, pale yellow, thick and shiny, which will take up to 35 minutes. You could also use an electric whisk if you prefer, as it will take less time. Meanwhile, soak the gelatin in cold water to cover until soft. Use your hands to squeeze out the water and to transfer the gelatin to the hot zabaglione. Mix until completely dissolved. (If using powdered gelatin, follow the maker's instructions for dissolving before adding to the zabaglione.) Be very careful not to let the zabaglione collapse in the process. Leave the zabaglione to cool completely, then fold in the whipped cream. Transfer to the refrigerator to chill and set until required.

Next, make the white chocolate mousse. Beat the egg yolks and the sugar together until pale yellow and thick. Melt the chocolate in a bowl placed over a pan of simmering water. When the chocolate is runny, cool it slightly by stirring it gently off the heat and then trickle it into the egg and sugar mixture, beating vigorously all the time. Set aside and turn your attention to the egg whites, which have been chilling. Place them in a clean, dry bowl and beat until they form stiff peaks. Mix 1 tablespoon of egg white into the chocolate mixture to slacken the mixture, then gently fold in the remaining egg white.

When all the egg white has been carefully folded through the mousse, start to layer up the dessert. If possible, use wide-stemmed glasses, or a pretty glass bowl. Begin by putting a layer of white chocolate mousse on the bottom, then a layer of zabaglione and so on until the glasses are filled. Chill until required, and then serve with the raspberries and amaretti cookies or *langues de chat*.

Crostata di Mele e Mandorle
Almond and Apple Tart

I like to use red-skinned apples to give this classic tart a lovely hint of color. By all means leave the tart in the tin to serve, if you are nervous about transferring it to a plate intact.

Serves 8
butter for greasing
¾ cup (200ml) light cream
6 tbsp superfine sugar
1 egg
1 cup (75g) ground almonds
3 dessert apples with red skin

For the pastry:
2⅔ cups (300g) all-purpose white flour, plus extra for dusting
½ cup (125g) superfine sugar
1¼ sticks unsalted butter
pinch of salt
1 egg yolk, beaten

To make the pastry, sift the flour onto the work surface with the sugar, then knead in the butter and salt with your fingertips to create a granular texture. Add the egg yolk and pull the pastry together into a ball, then wrap in plastic wrap and refrigerate for 30 minutes.

Butter and flour a 8½-in (22-cm) pie pan with a removeable base; set aside.

Mix the cream with the sugar, egg, and the ground almonds; set aside. Rinse and dry the apples, then core and slice them thinly.

Roll out the pastry on a lightly floured work surface and use to line the prepared pie pan. Arrange the sliced apples in the pastry shell in slightly overlapping circles. Pour the cream mixture over the apples to cover.

Place the tart in a preheated oven, 50°F, and bake for 45 minutes until golden and set. Leave the tart to cool completely on a wire rack before removing from the pan and serving.

Frappe
Frappe

Traditionally served at Carnival time, these dry, sweet, and very light cookies are a perfect end to a heavy meal at any time of the year when served with a bottle of chilled dessert wine.

Makes about 1lb (500g)
about 3½ cups (500g) all-purpose white flour, plus extra for rolling out
25g (1oz) lard, or vegetable fat
1 whole egg
2 extra yolks
1 tbsp sugar
pinch of salt
a glass or so of white wine
sunflower oil for deep-fat frying
confectioners' sugar for dusting
chilled vin santo or other dessert wine to, serve

Mix together the flour, lard, egg, egg yolks, sugar, and salt. Gradually add enough wine to make a soft ball of dough, not dissimilar to fresh pasta dough. Gather the dough into a ball, wrap in plastic wrap and leave to rest for about 30 minutes at room temperature. Roll out the dough on a lightly floured surface until thin, then cut into the desired shapes, usually longish wide ribbons.

Heat the oil in a wide pan until a small square of bread dropped into the oil sizzles instantly. Carefully drop a few pieces of dough into the oil at a time, about 6 or 7 in each batch. As soon as they puff up, become golden and are floating on the surface, scoop them out with a slotted spoon and drain on paper towels. Continue until all the dough is fried. Dust with confectioners' sugar and serve warm with chilled vin santo or other dessert wine.

Semifreddo al Miele e Arance

Honey and Orange *Semifreddo*

Semifreddo always makes a very simple but impressive dessert. This one is sweet and tangy, slightly boozy and melts to a deliciously soft texture.

2 large unwaxed oranges
5 egg yolks
5 tbsp orange blossom honey
2 tbsp Curaçao or Grand Marnier
2 cups (500ml) whipping cream
1 cup (125g) toasted almonds

Grate the rind from one orange and set aside. Beat the egg yolks with an electric mixer, gradually adding the honey in a thin stream until the mixture is pale and foaming.

Carefully fold in the grated orange rind and the liqueur. In a separate bowl, whip the cream until stiff peaks form, then slowly and gently fold it into the egg and honey mixture.

Pour the mixture into a lidded, bowl-shaped mold, cover and freeze for about 3 hours. Meanwhile, slice half of the whole orange into neat, thin slices. Slice the skin of the other half into neat, narrow strips, removing all the pith. Take the *semifreddo* out of the freezer and let it stand for about 10 minutes, then turn it out on to a platter. Decorate the sides and the top with the almonds and garnish with the sliced orange and the sliced orange peel. Serve.

Gelato di Cocomero

Watermelon Ice Cream

The Sicilians invented ice cream, having been taught how to make the original version of this universal dessert by their Arab invaders. Nowhere in the world will you taste ice cream quite like Sicilian ice cream, which is amazingly fragrant and very special indeed. This recipe will just give you a basic idea of what I mean. Please make sure you use a really sweet, ripe watermelon.

Serves 8–10
1lb (500g) watermelon flesh, weighed without skin or seeds
1½ cups (300g) superfine sugar
2 tbsp jasmine flower water or 2 tsp orange blossom water
3½oz (100g) best quality Continental dark chocolate, finely chopped
½ cup (50g) unsalted pistachio nuts, chopped
3½oz (100g) candied pumpkin or citrus, chopped
1 tsp ground cinnamon

Push the watermelon flesh through a sieve and mix it thoroughly with half the sugar and the jasmine flower water. Pour it into a mold, cover tightly with a lid to help prevent crystals and freeze until slushy, stirring every 10 minutes or so to break up any ice crystals. When the mixture is thick and slushy, stir in the chocolate, the remaining sugar, the nuts, candied pumpkin or citrus, and the cinnamon. Return to the freezer and continue to freeze until solid, stirring occasionally.

When you are ready to serve, dip the mold into hot water to loosen the edges, then turn out onto a platter and serve at once.

Spumone di Fragole

Sicilian Strawberry Ice Cream

In the great hierarchy of Italian ice cream, the *spumone* sits somewhere between the *gelato* and the *semifreddo*. This is a real classic from my childhood.

Serves 6

1lb (500g) strawberries, rinsed and hulled

5 tbsp fresh ricotta or thick heavy cream (for a much richer finish)

freshly squeezed juice of ½ lemon

2 cups (500ml) whipping cream

1¼ cups (150g) confectioners' sugar

12 large strawberries, sliced, or 2 handfuls wild strawberries, left whole, rinsed and dried

To serve:

extra strawberries

fresh mint leaves

strawberry-flavored liqueur or reduced balsamic vinegar (see page 80)

Push the strawberries through a sieve or whiz in a food processor to make a purée. Mix in the ricotta or thick cream, then add the lemon juice, stirring quickly to prevent curdling.

Whip the cream until stiff, and then gently sift over the confectioners' sugar and fold it in very gradually and carefully. Fold the sweetened cream into the strawberry purée. Finally, fold through the sliced or wild strawberries.

Pour the mixture into a plastic freezerproof container with a lid and freeze for about 2 hours, stirring 2 or 3 times during the freezing process to prevent any substantial ice crystals forming, although the slightly gritty texture of this dessert is correct and typical of a *spumone*, so don't worry if you end up with a few small crystals.

To serve, take the *spumone* out of the refrigerator and leave to stand for up to 15 minutes to soften. Dip the mold into boiling hot water for 10 seconds, then invert on to a platter, remove the mold and cut into 6 slices. Place each slice on a plate with a few strawberries, a sprig of mint leaves, and a drizzle of strawberry liqueur or reduced balsamic vinegar. Serve immediately.

Crema pasticciera

Custard

Serve this delicious egg custard with the Cassata on page 124, or the Apple Charlotte opposite.

Serves 6

5 egg yolks

⅔ cup (150g) superfine sugar

2 cups (500ml) whole milk

2 tsp vanilla extract

Beat the egg yolks and the sugar together until light, fluffy, and foaming.

Bring the milk to just under boiling point—do not allow it to boil. Gradually strain the milk into the egg yolk and sugar mixture, beating constantly. Never add any more milk until the previous amount has been absorbed into the egg yolk mixture.

Return to the heat and reheat, stirring constantly. Again, don't allow the mixture to boil. When it is thickened enough that it will coat the back of a spoon, stir in the vanilla extract and remove from the heat.

Strain and cool completely, covering the top with a little cream or cold milk to prevent a skin from forming, or cover the surface with a piece of plastic wrap.

Charlotte di Mele
Apple Charlotte

A classic recipe from the Lombardy region, very old fashioned and completely delicious.

Serves 8
2lb (1kg) dessert apples
1lb (500g) sliced white bread, thinly
buttered on each side
½ cup (100g) granulated sugar
½ tsp ground cinnamon
3 tbsp pine nuts
2 tbsp chopped candied fruit
4 cups (1 liter) prepared egg custard
(see page 138)
a few dots of unsalted butter, plus a little
for greasing
sweetened mascarpone cheese, whipped,
or light cream for serving

Butter a deep ovenproof dish large enough to hold all the ingredients; set aside.

Peel and slice all the apples thinly. Arrange a layer of buttered bread across the base of the prepared dish. Sprinkle with sugar and add a layer of apples, then a sprinkling each of cinnamon, pine nuts, and candied fruit. Cover with custard and repeat until the ingredients have all been used. Finish with a few dots of butter.

Place the dish in a preheated oven, 350°F, and bake for about 30–40 minutes or until browned and set. Serve warm, with a dollop of mascarpone or light cream.

Torta di Polenta
Polenta Cake

If you make this cake a couple of days before you want to eat it, it will become quite hard and thus be perfect for dunking languorously into a glass of sweet dessert wine at the end of a long, relaxed meal.

Makes one 9½-in (24-cm) cake
oil for greasing
¼ cup (25g) golden raisins
8oz (250g) fresh ricotta
2 cups (500ml) tepid water
½ cup (125g) sugar
1⅛ cups (250g) fine polenta
1 tsp ground cinnamon

Grease a shallow 9½-in (24-cm) cake pan; set aside. Cover the golden raisins with warm water and leave to soak for about 30 minutes, then drain and dry with care.

Dilute the ricotta with the water, beating vigorously with a balloon whisk. Beat in the sugar, then add the polenta in a fine stream very gradually to avoid lumps. Add the cinnamon and the sultanas and give the cake one final stir.

Pour the polenta mixture into the prepared cake pan and bang it down gently to remove any air bubbles. Place in a preheated oven, 350°F, and bake for about 1 hour or until the cake is firm and a knife inserted into the center comes out clean. Leave to cool slightly, then serve warm, straight from the pan, or leave to cool completely.

index

Page numbers in *italics* indicate illustrations.